Guided Reading and Study Workbook (Level A)

Prentice Hall

Earth Science

Boston, Massachusetts
Upper Saddle River, New Jersey

Guided Reading and Study Workbook (Level A)

Prentice Hall

Earth Science

13-digit ISBN 978-0-13-362761-9
10-digit ISBN 0-13-362761-6

21 18

Contents

Name ______________________ Class ________________ Date ____________

Chapter 1 Introduction to Earth Science

Section 1.1 What Is Earth Science?

This section explains what Earth science is and what Earth scientists study.

Reading Strategy

Categorizing As you read about the different branches of Earth science, fill in the column with the name of each branch and list some of the things that are studied. For more information on this Reading Strategy, see the **Reading and Study Skills** in the **Skills and Reference Handbook** at the end of your textbook.

geology	a.
b.	c.
d.	e.
f.	g.

Overview of Earth Science

1. Circle the letters of the topics studied in Earth science.
   a. Earth's atmosphere
   b. Earth's surface
   c. Earth's neighbors in space
   d. Earth's interior
2. What are some of the subdivisions of Earth science? ______________________
3. What does the word *geology* mean? ______________________
4. Is the following sentence true or false? Geology is divided into two broad areas—physical geology and historical geology. ______________
5. What do physical geologists study? ______________________
6. Rocks and minerals form in response to Earth's ______________ and ______________ processes.

7. What do historical geologists study? ______________________________

8. Circle the letter of each science that is integrated into oceanography.
   a. chemistry
   b. biology
   c. physics
   d. meteorology

9. What do oceanographers study? ______________________________

10. The study of the atmosphere and the processes that produce weather and climate is ________________.

11. The science of ________________ is the study of the universe.

Formation of Earth

12. The ________________ hypothesis suggests that the bodies of our solar system evolved from an enormous rotating cloud called the solar nebula.

13. Is the following sentence true or false? The solar nebula is made up of mostly carbon and iron. ________________

14. Look at the diagram. Describe what is occurring in the first two stages of the formation of the solar system according to the nebular hypothesis.

Name ______________________ Class ________________ Date ___________

Section 1.2 A View of Earth

This section explains the physical structure of Earth.

Reading Strategy

Predicting Before you read, predict the meaning of the vocabulary terms. After you read, revise your definition if your prediction was incorrect. For more information on this Reading Strategy, see the **Reading and Study Skills** in the **Skills and Reference Handbook** at the end of your textbook.

Vocabulary Term	Before You Read	After You Read
hydrosphere	a.	b.
atmosphere	c.	d.
geosphere	e.	f.
biosphere	g.	h.
core	i.	j.
mantle	k.	l.
crust	m.	n.

Earth's Major Spheres

1. Earth can be thought of as consisting of four major spheres: the ________________, ________________, ________________, and ________________.

Match each term to its description.

	Term	**Description**
_____	**2.** hydrosphere	a. all life-forms on Earth
_____	**3.** atmosphere	b. composed of the core, mantle, and crust
_____	**4.** geosphere	c. dense, heavy inner sphere of Earth
_____	**5.** biosphere	d. thin outside layer of Earth's surface
_____	**6.** core	e. the water portion of Earth
_____	**7.** mantle	f. the gaseous envelope around Earth
_____	**8.** crust	g. located between the crust and core of Earth

9. What does each letter in the diagram below represent?

A. ______________
B. ______________
C. ______________
D. ______________
E. ______________
F. ______________
G. ______________
H. ______________
I. ______________
J. ______________

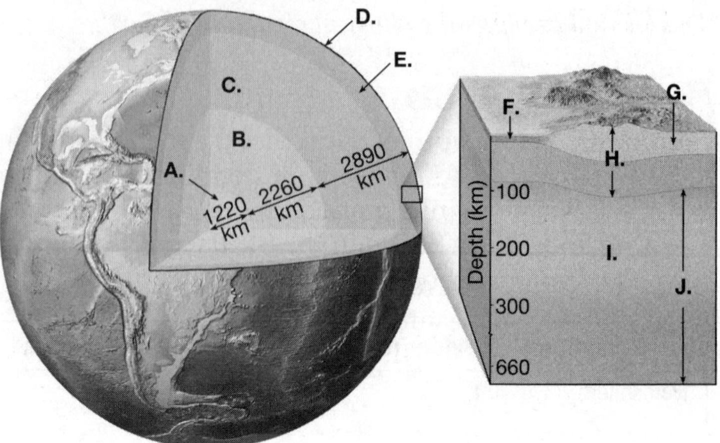

Plate Tectonics

10. Is the following sentence true or false? Forces such as weathering and erosion that work to wear away high points and flatten out Earth's surface are called constructive forces. ______________

11. Circle the letter of each type of constructive force.
    a. gravity
    b. mountain building
    c. ocean currents
    d. volcanism

12. Is the following sentence true or false? Constructive forces depend on Earth's internal heat for their source of energy.
    ____

13. Circle the letter of the theory that provided geologists with a model to explain how earthquakes and volcanic eruptions occur and how continents move.
    a. continental drift
    b. evolution
    c. plate tectonics
    d. Pangaea

14. Explain the principles of the plate tectonics theory. ______________

____

____

____

____

____

____

____

____

Name ____________ Class ____________ Date ____________

Section 1.3 Representing Earth's Surface

This section explains various types of globes and maps used to represent Earth's surface.

Reading Strategy

Monitoring Your Understanding Preview the Key Concepts, topic headings, vocabulary, and figures in this section. List two things you expect to learn. After reading, state what you learned about each item you listed. For more information on this Reading Strategy, see the **Reading and Study Skills** in the **Skills and Reference Handbook** at the end of your textbook.

What I Expect to Learn	What I Learned
a.	b.
c.	d.

Determining Location

Match each description to its term.

Description

_____ **1.** the distance north or south of the equator

_____ **2.** the distance east or west of the prime meridian

_____ **3.** the line of latitude around the middle of the globe at 0 degrees

_____ **4.** the line of longitude at 0 degrees

_____ **5.** the two hemispheres formed by the equator

_____ **6.** the two hemispheres formed by the prime meridian and the 180° meridian

_____ **7.** a spherical model of Earth

Term

a. longitude
b. globe
c. eastern, western
d. prime meridian
e. northern, southern
f. latitude
g. equator

Maps and Mapping

8. A(n) ______________________ is a flat representation of Earth's surface.

9. Match the name of the map type with the correct example below.

Robinson Projection   Mercator Projection
Gnomonic Projection   Conic Projection

A. ______________________

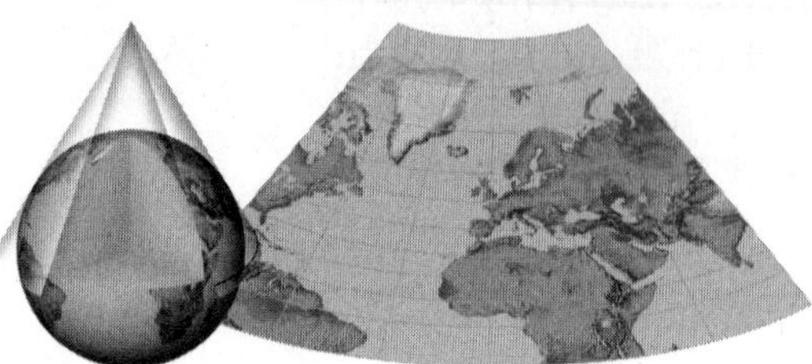

B. ______________________

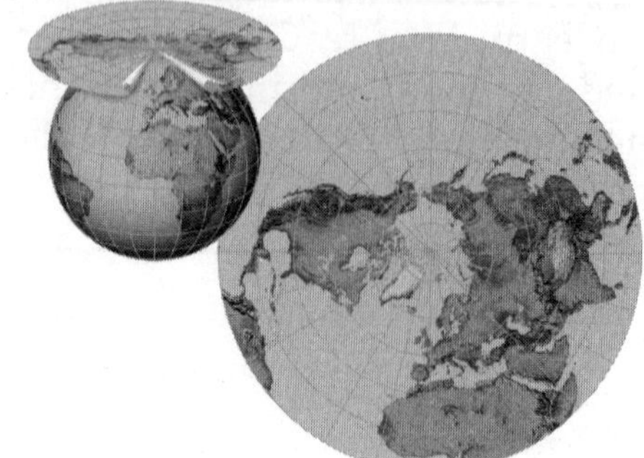

C. ______________________

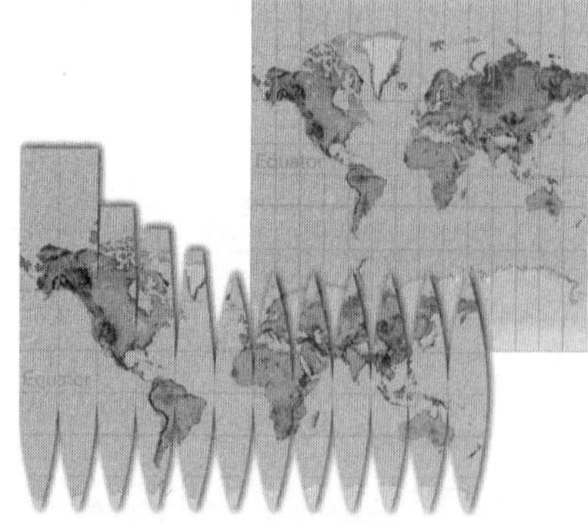

D. ______________________

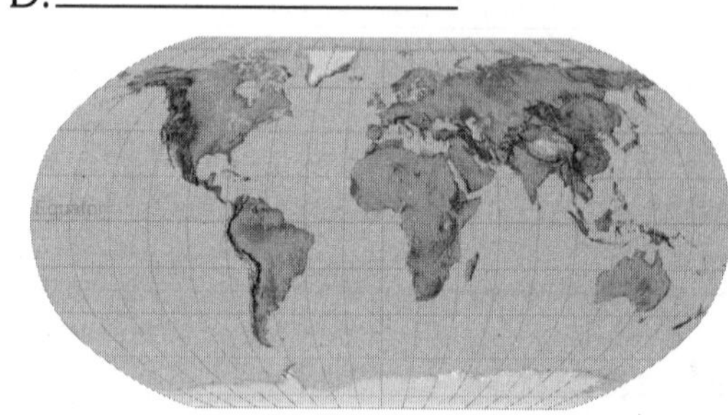

Topographic Maps

10. Circle the information that topographical maps show.

a. the round shape of Earth with no distortion
b. the depth of Earth's layers
c. separations between different climates
d. the elevation of Earth's surface

Advanced Technology

11. Is the following sentence true or false? The process of collecting data about Earth from a distance (such as from orbiting satellites) is called remote sensing. ______________________

12. Circle the things scientists can study using satellite remote sensing.

a. rivers and oceans   b. fires
c. pollution   d. natural resources

Name ______________________ Class ________________ Date ____________

Section 1.4 Earth System Science

This section describes Earth as a system of interacting parts.

Reading Strategy

Outlining As you read, make an outline of the most important ideas in this section. Begin with the section title, then list the green headings as the next step of the outline. Outline further as needed. For more information on this Reading Strategy, see the **Reading and Study Skills** in the **Skills and Reference Handbook** at the end of your textbook.

I. Earth System Science
   A. What Is a System?
      1. ______________________________
         ____
      2. ______________________________
         ____
   B. ______________________________
      1. ______________________________
         ____
      2. ______________________________
         ____
         ____

1. Earth is a(n) ________________ made up of numerous interacting parts, or subsystems.

What Is a System?

2. A system can be any size group of interacting parts that form a complex ________________.

3. What is a closed system? ______________________________

____

____

____

4. What is an open system? ______________________________

____

____

Earth as a System

5. Is the following sentence true or false? The Earth system is powered by energy from the sun and Earth's exterior.

____

6. Is the following sentence true or false? The sun drives external processes that occur in the atmosphere, hydrosphere, and at Earth's surface. ________________

7. Complete the concept map below.

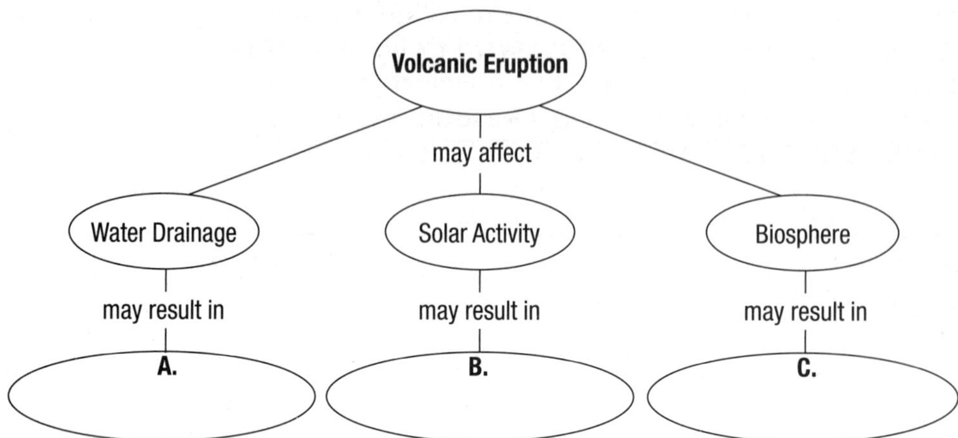

People and the Environment

8. Circle the letter of each statement that is true about nonliving things that make up the environment.
   a. Water and air are nonliving things that make up the environment.
   b. Plants, animals, and microscopic organisms are nonliving things that make up the environment.
   c. Temperature, humidity, and sunlight are conditions that make up the environment.
   d. Soil and rock are nonliving things that make up the environment.

9. What are renewable resources? ____

____

____

____

____

10. Circle the letter of each item that is a nonrenewable resource.
   a. iron
   b. petroleum
   c. aluminum
   d. natural fibers

Environmental Problems

11. Significant threats to the environment include ________________, ________________, ________________, and ________________.

Section 1.5 What Is Scientific Inquiry?

This section describes methods used for scientific inquiry.

Reading Strategy

Comparing and Contrasting As you read, complete the Venn diagram by listing the ways that a hypothesis and a theory are alike and how they differ. For more information on this Reading Strategy, see the **Reading and Study Skills** in the **Skills and Reference Handbook** at the end of your textbook.

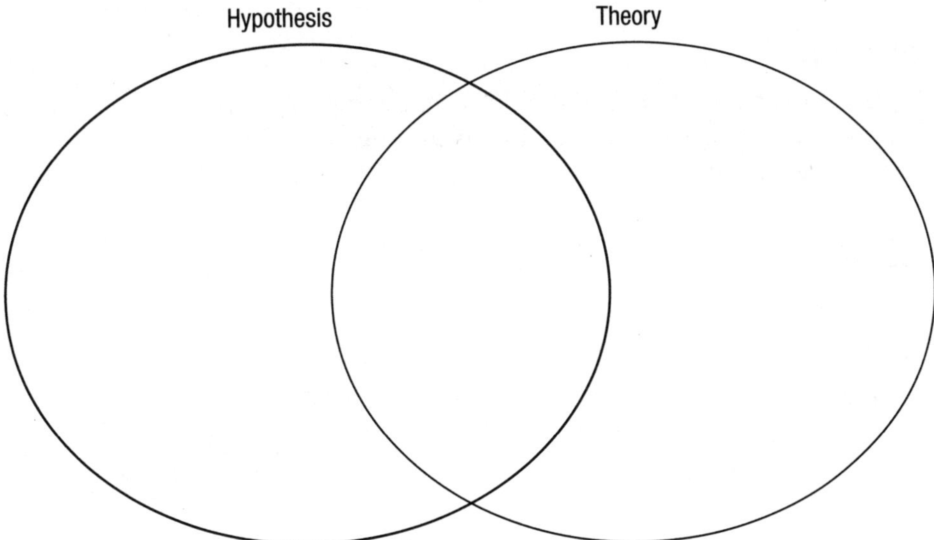

Hypothesis

1. What is a hypothesis? ______________________________

____

2. Is the following sentence true or false? Before a hypothesis can become an accepted part of scientific knowledge, it must be tested and analyzed. ______________

3. Describe a well-known hypothesis that was discarded because it was found to be untrue. ______________________________

____

____

4. Circle the letter of each sentence that is true about hypotheses.
   a. If a hypothesis can't be tested, it is not scientifically useful.
   b. Hypotheses that fail rigorous testing are discarded.
   c. A hypothesis is a well-tested and widely accepted principle.
   d. The concept of plate tectonics is a hypothesis.

5. Is the following sentence true or false? Sometimes more than one hypothesis is developed to explain the same set of observations.

____

Theory

6. A scientific _______________ is well tested and widely accepted by the scientific community and best explains certain observable facts.

7. Describe a scientific theory that is currently accepted as true. _______________

____

____

____

____

Scientific Methods

8. Circle the letter that best answers the question. What is the process of gathering facts through observations and formulating scientific hypotheses and theories called?

   a. scientific hypothesis

   b. scientific theory

   c. scientific method

   d. scientific testing

9. Complete the flowchart showing the basic steps of the scientific method.

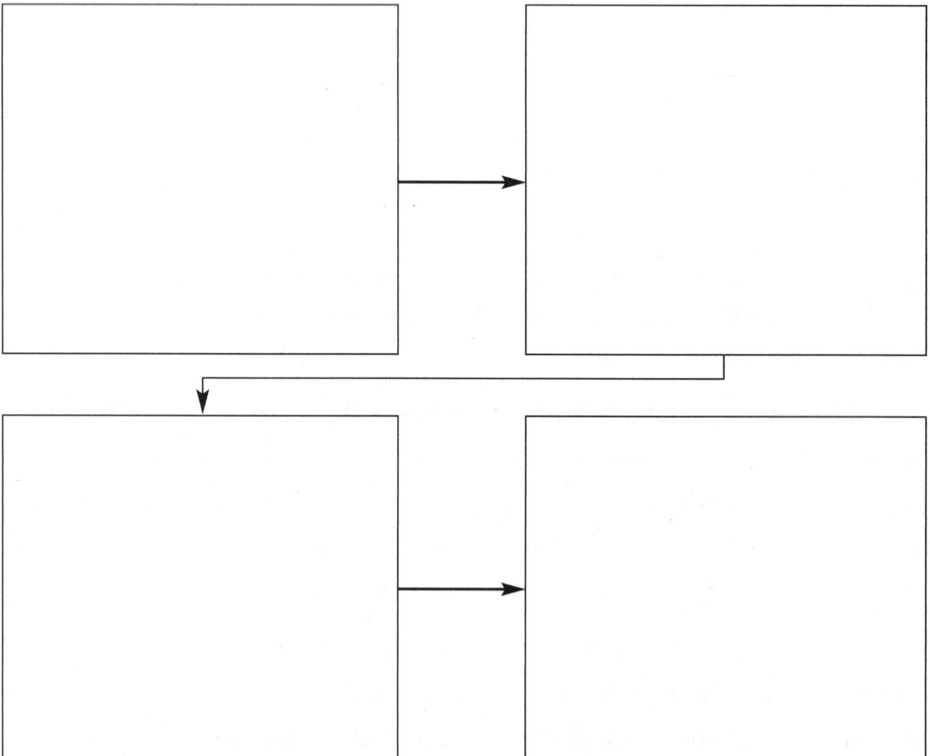

10. Is the following sentence true or false? All scientists follow the same steps outlined above when doing scientific research.

____

Name ____________________ Class ____________________ Date ____________

WordWise

Complete the sentences by using the scrambled vocabulary terms below.

troasnmyo	ymteeogorlo	tmsaohpeer
ttldeaiu	tidelngou	coountr lavterin
eoghpsree	ncoourt ilnes	essithopyh
yggeool	gocoaitprph pma	mstyes
oieepshbr	yhdroeeshrp	traeh ncsiece

The name of the group of sciences that deal with Earth and its neighbors in space is called ____________________.

All the water on Earth makes up the ____________________.

A word that means "study of Earth" is ____________________.

A distance measured in degrees north or south of the equator is called ____________________.

A distance measured in degrees east or west of the prime meridian is called ____________________.

The ____________________ tells you the difference in elevation between two adjacent lines on a topographic map.

Lying beneath both the atmosphere and the ocean is the ____________________.

A ____________________ can be any size group of interacting parts that form a complex whole.

An untested scientific explanation is called a ____________________.

The gaseous envelope surrounding Earth is called the ____________________.

A ____________________ represents Earth's three-dimensional surface in two dimensions.

The elevation on a topographic map is shown using ____________________.

The ____________________ includes all life on Earth.

The study of the atmosphere and the processes that produce weather and climate is ____________________.

The study of the universe is ____________________.

Section 2.1 Matter

This section discusses the relationship between minerals and elements. It explains the parts of an atom and defines ions, isotopes, compounds, and chemical bonds.

Reading Strategy

Comparing and Contrasting As you read, complete the organizer to compare and contrast protons, neutrons, and electrons. For more information on this Reading Strategy, see the **Reading and Study Skills** in the **Skills and Reference Handbook** at the end of your textbook.

	Protons	Electrons	Neutrons
Differences			
Similarities			

Elements and the Periodic Table

1. A substance that cannot be broken down into simpler substances by chemical or physical means is called a(n) ____________________.

2. The document in which elements are organized by their properties is known as the ____________________.

3. Circle the letter of the name for the columns within the periodic table.
   a. periods
   b. groups
   c. metals
   d. compounds

Atoms

4. What is an atom? ____

5. The atomic number of boron is 5. What does this tell you about an atom of boron?
____
____

6. Name the three main types of particles in an atom.

____

7. Indicate where each type of particle is located in an atom by placing the first letter of each name on the diagram.

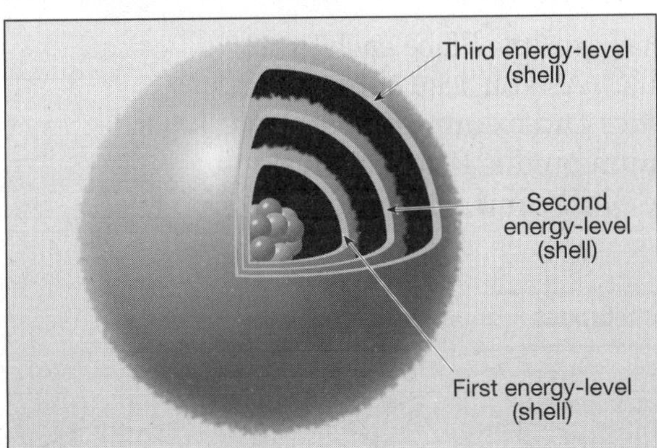

8. From which energy level in the diagram would atomic particles be transferred to form a compound? ______________

Isotopes

9. Is the following sentence true or false? Isotopes of carbon have the same number of neutrons and different numbers of protons.

____

10. Is the following sentence true or false? The total mass of an atom of nitrogen is known as the atom's mass number. ______________

Why Atoms Bond

11. What does a compound consist of? ____

____

12. What is likely to happen to an atom of oxygen that does not contain the maximum number of electrons in its outermost energy level? ____

____

Types of Chemical Bonds

Match each description with its type of chemical bond.

Description	Chemical Bond
______ 13. when one metal ion shares electrons with another metal ion	a. covalent
______ 14. when a positive ion is attracted to a negative ion	b. ionic
______ 15. when one atom shares electrons with another atom	c. metallic

Section 2.2 Minerals

This section explains what minerals are and how they are formed, classified, and grouped.

Reading Strategy

Previewing Skim the material on mineral groups. Place each group name into one of the ovals in the organizer. As you read this section, complete the organizer with characteristics and examples of each major mineral group. For more information on this Reading Strategy, see the **Reading and Study Skills** in the **Skills and Reference Handbook** at the end of your textbook.

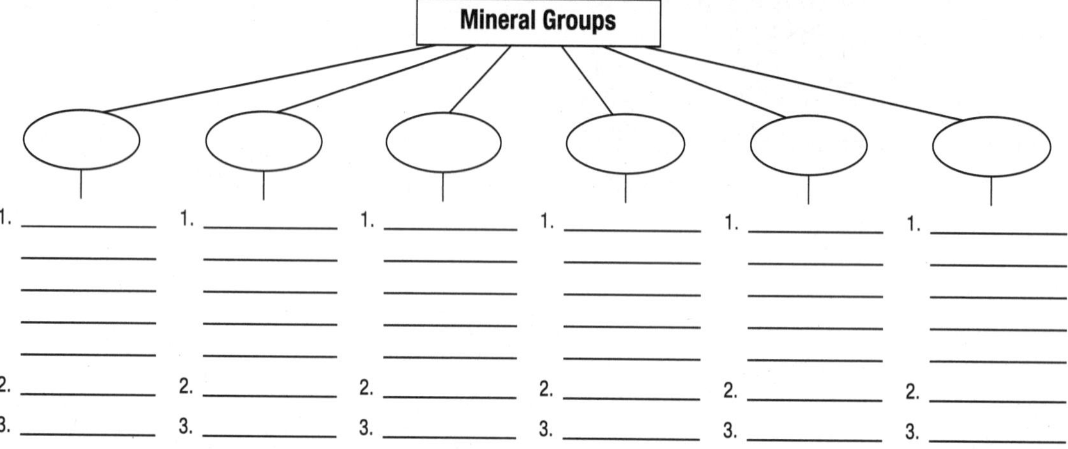

Describe the five characteristics an Earth material must have to be called a mineral.

1. ____

2. ____

3. ____

4. ____

5. ____

Name ______________ Class ______________ Date ______________

How Minerals Form

Match each description with its process of mineral formation.

	Description	Process of Mineral Formation
_____	6. As molten rock cools, elements combine to form minerals.	a. hydrothermal solution
_____	7. Existing minerals recrystallize while still solid under pressure or form new minerals when temperature changes.	b. pressure and temperature changes
_____	8 Hot mixtures of water and dissolved substances react with existing minerals to form new minerals.	c. precipitation
_____	9. Substances dissolved in water react to form new minerals when the water evaporates.	d. crystallization from magma

Mineral Groups

10. What property is used to classify minerals into groups such as silicates? ______________

11. What is the structure shown in the diagram? ______________

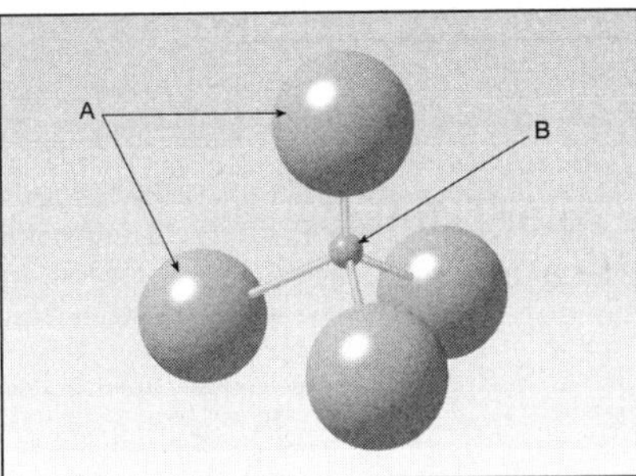

12. In the diagram, letter A identifies ______________ atoms.

13. In the diagram, letter B identifies a(n) ______________ atom.

14. Circle the letter of something common to all halides.
    a. an oxygen ion
    b. the element sulfur
    c. a metallic element
    d. a halogen ion

15. Circle the letter of the mineral group whose members only contain one element.
    a. native elements
    b. sulfates
    c. carbonates
    d. oxides

16. Is the following sentence true or false? Both carbonates and oxides are minerals that contain the element oxygen.

____

Name ______________________ Class ________________ Date ____________

Chapter 2 Minerals

Section 2.3 Properties of Minerals

This section discusses the properties used to identify minerals, including color, luster, crystal form, streak, hardness, density, and some distinctive properties.

Reading Strategy

Outlining As you read, fill in the outline. Use the headings as the main topics and add supporting details. For more information on this Reading Strategy, see the **Reading and Study Skills** in the **Skills and Reference Handbook** at the end of your textbook.

I. Properties of Minerals
   A. Color
      1. ______________________
      2. ______________________
   B. Luster
      1. ______________________
      2. ______________________

Color

1. Is the following sentence true or false? Because color is unique to all minerals, it is always useful in mineral identification. ______________

Streak

2. The color of a mineral in its ______________ form is called streak.

Luster

3. What is a mineral's luster? ______________________

4. Circle the letter of the type of luster some minerals have that makes them appear to be metals.
   a. earthy
   b. sub-metallic
   c. metallic
   d. glassy

Crystal Form

5. Is the following sentence true or false? The visible expression of a mineral's internal arrangement of atoms is its crystal form. ______________

Hardness

6. Circle the letter of the hardest mineral shown on the graph.
   a. talc
   b. diamond
   c. topaz
   d. quartz

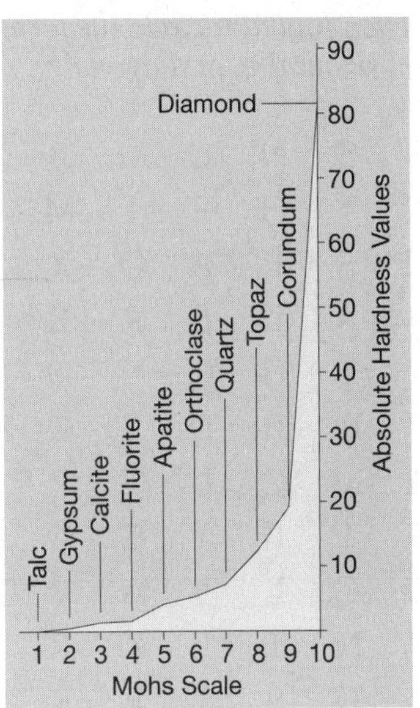

7. Circle the letter of the hardness number of corundum on the Mohs scale shown on the graph.
   a. 7
   b. 9
   c. 10
   d. 20

8. Circle the letter of the mineral that is harder than apatite shown on the graph.
   a. talc
   b. calcite
   c. fluorite
   d. orthoclase

Cleavage

9. What is a mineral's cleavage? ____

____

____

Fracture

10. Minerals are said to ____________________ if they do not show cleavage when broken.

Density

11. What equation could you use to express the density of an object such as a mineral sample? ______________________________

Distinctive Properties of Minerals

12. Circle the letter of the distinctive property you could use to distinguish graphite from talc.
    a. color
    b. feel
    c. double refraction
    d. smell

Name ______________________ Class ________________ Date ____________

Chapter 2 Minerals

WordWise

Solve the clues to determine which vocabulary terms from Chapter 2 are hidden in the puzzle. Then find and circle the terms in the puzzle. The terms may occur vertically, horizontally, or diagonally.

V	E	M	A	S	S	N	U	M	B	E	R	U	N
C	D	Y	S	X	T	H	E	I	M	G	N	G	I
W	M	E	J	H	S	P	A	Q	X	Z	I	O	S
M	I	N	E	R	A	L	S	R	E	U	Y	J	O
S	C	E	H	V	T	H	Q	N	D	A	E	I	T
A	X	R	Y	P	O	B	D	T	C	N	S	L	O
L	I	G	R	A	M	C	U	G	P	L	E	S	P
B	A	Y	C	S	I	L	I	C	A	T	E	S	E
T	K	L	F	U	C	L	E	A	V	A	G	E	S
M	I	E	G	X	N	T	E	K	P	H	T	E	P
A	D	V	U	L	U	S	T	E	R	Z	P	J	B
C	H	E	L	E	M	E	N	T	D	S	S	T	X
E	X	L	M	N	B	A	U	S	S	V	H	A	L
Z	P	S	B	C	E	W	R	T	N	O	H	I	A
R	G	C	D	Q	R	J	H	S	M	F	L	K	P

Clues	Hidden Words
How light is reflected from the surface of a mineral	______________
Number of protons in an atom of an element	______________
Atoms of the same element having different numbers of neutrons	______________
Measure of how a mineral resists scratching	______________
Substance that cannot be broken down into simpler substances	______________
Examples include quartz, copper, fluorite, and talc	______________
Regions where electrons are located	______________
Most common groups of minerals on Earth	______________
Tendency of a mineral to break along flat, even surfaces	______________
Sum of protons and neutrons in the nucleus of an atom	______________

Name ______________________ Class ______________ Date __________

Chapter 3 Rocks

Section 3.1 The Rock Cycle

This section explains the different types of rocks found on Earth and in the rock cycle.

Reading Strategy

Building Vocabulary As you read, write down the definition for each term. For more information on this Reading Strategy, see the **Reading and Study Skills** in the **Skills and Reference Handbook** at the end of your textbook.

Term	Definition
rock	a.
igneous rock	b.
sedimentary rock	c.
metamorphic rock	d.
rock cycle	e.
magma	f.
lava	g.
weathering	h.
sediment	i.

Rocks

1. A(n) ______________ is any solid mass of mineral or mineral-like matter that occurs naturally as part of Earth.

2. Most rocks, such as granite, occur as a solid mixture of ______________.

3. Is the following sentence true or false? A characteristic of rock is that each of the component minerals retains its properties in the mixture. ______________

4. Describe a few rocks that are composed of nonmineral matter. ______________

____

____

____

5. Circle the letters that identify a type of rock.
   a. igneous
   b. sedimentary
   c. metamorphic
   d. crystalline

The Rock Cycle

6. Fill in the blanks below in the illustration of the rock cycle.

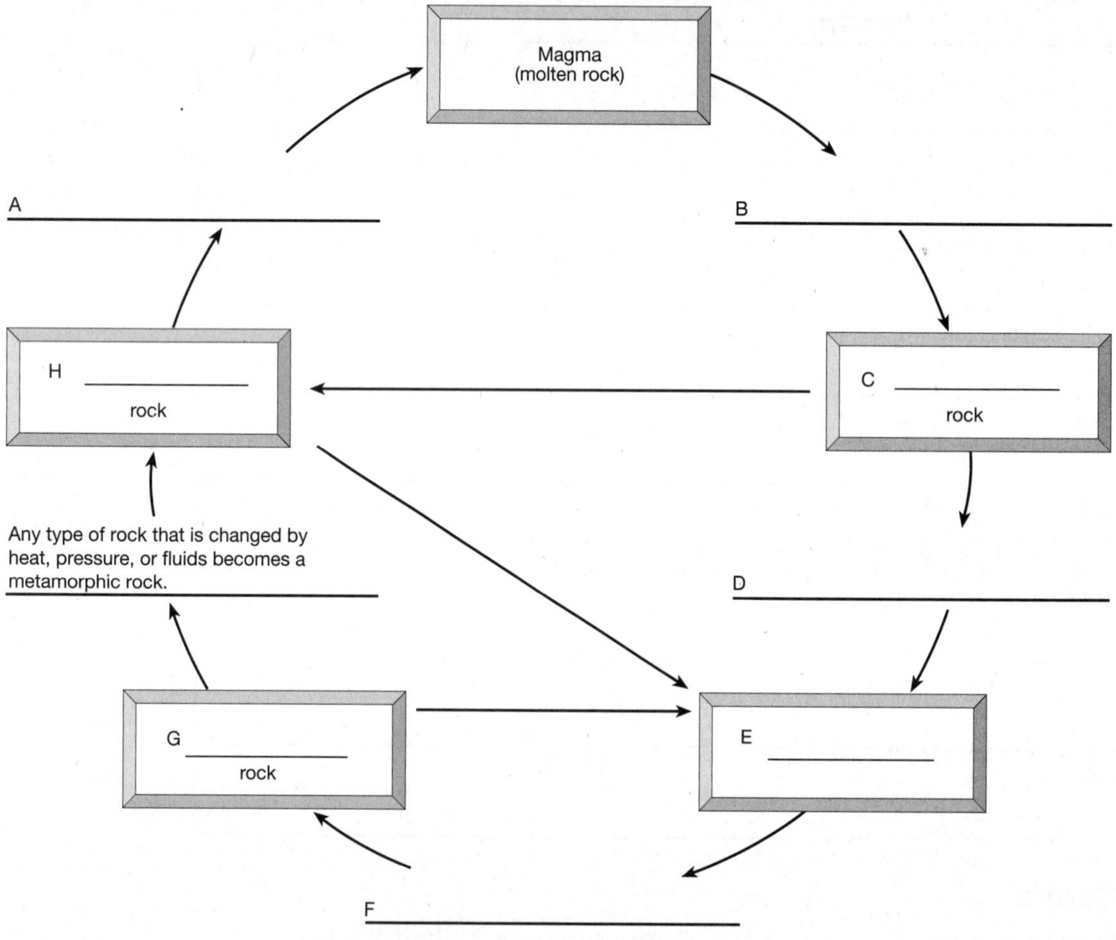

Alternate Paths

7. Give an example of an alternate path in the rock cycle.

____

____

____

____

____

Name ______________________ Class ________________ Date ___________

Chapter 3 Rocks

Section 3.2 Igneous Rocks

This section discusses the characteristics of igneous rocks.

Reading Strategy

Outlining Complete the outline as you read. Include points about how each of these rocks form, some of the characteristics of each rock type, and some examples of each. For more information on this Reading Strategy, see the **Reading and Study Skills** in the **Skills and Reference Handbook** at the end of your textbook.

I. Igneous Rocks
   A. Intrusive Rocks
      1. ______________________
      2. ______________________
   B. Extrusive Rocks
      1. ______________________
      2. ______________________

Formation of Igneous Rocks

Match each description to its term.

	Description	Term
_____	**1.** the meaning of the Latin word *ignis*	a. magma
_____	**2.** rocks that form when magma hardens beneath Earth's surface	b. granite
_____	**3.** rocks that form when lava hardens	c. intrusive igneous
_____	**4.** melted material beneath Earth's surface	d. lava
_____	**5.** melted material at Earth's surface	e. rhyolite
_____	**6.** an intrusive igneous rock that forms when magma cools slowly beneath Earth's surface	f. fire
_____	**7.** an extrusive igneous rock that forms when lava cools quickly at Earth's surface	g. extrusive igneous

8. Complete the table below.

Compare and Contrast Igneous Rocks		
	Granite	**Rhyolite**
Compare		
Contrast		

Classification of Igneous Rocks

9. Two characteristics used to classify igneous rocks are ________________ and ________________.

10. Is the following sentence true or false? Igneous rocks that are composed primarily of quartz and feldspar have a granitic composition. ________________

11. Rocks that contain dark silicate minerals and plagioclase feldspar have a(n) ________________.

12. Circle the letters of the minerals that are found in andesitic rocks.
    a. amphibole
    b. pyroxene
    c. biotite
    d. plagioclase feldspar

13. Peridotite is composed almost entirely of dark silicate minerals. Its chemical composition is referred to as ________________.

14. Is the following sentence true or false? Much of the upper mantle is thought to be made of granite. ________________

15. Circle the statements that are true about the texture of igneous rocks.
    a. Slow cooling results in rocks with small, interconnected mineral grains.
    b. Rapid cooling of magma or lava results in rocks with small, interconnected mineral grains.
    c. A glassy texture is the result of lava that has cooled very slowly.
    d. An even rate of cooling results in rocks with very different-sized minerals.

Name ______________ Class ______________ Date ______________

Section 3.3 Sedimentary Rocks

This section discusses the formation and classification of sedimentary rocks.

Reading Strategy

Outlining This outline is a continuation of the outline from Section 3.2. Complete this outline as you read. Include points about how each of these rocks forms, some of the characteristics of each rock type, and some examples of each. For more information on this Reading Strategy, see the **Reading and Study Skills** in the **Skills and Reference Handbook** at the end of your textbook.

II. Sedimentary Rocks
- A. Clastic Rocks
  1. ______________
  2. ______________
- B. Chemical Rocks
  1. ______________
  2. ______________

Formation of Sedimentary Rocks

Match each description to its term.

	Description	Term
_____	**1.** a process that squeezes, or compacts, sediments	a. cementation
_____	**2.** involves weathering and the removal of rock	b. deposition
_____	**3.** takes place when dissolved minerals are deposited in the tiny spaces among the sediments	c. compaction
_____	**4.** when sediments are dropped by water, wind, ice, or gravity	d. erosion

5. Is the following sentence true or false? Sedimentary rocks form when solids settle out of a fluid such as water or air.

____

6. Circle the letters of the statements that are true of the formation of sedimentary rocks.
   a. Weathering is the first step in the formation of sedimentary rocks.
   b. Weathered sediments don't usually remain in place.
   c. Small sediments often are carried large distances before being deposited.
   d. Small sediments usually are deposited first.

Classification of Sedimentary Rocks

7. Complete the Venn diagram comparing the formation of the two main groups of sedimentary rocks.

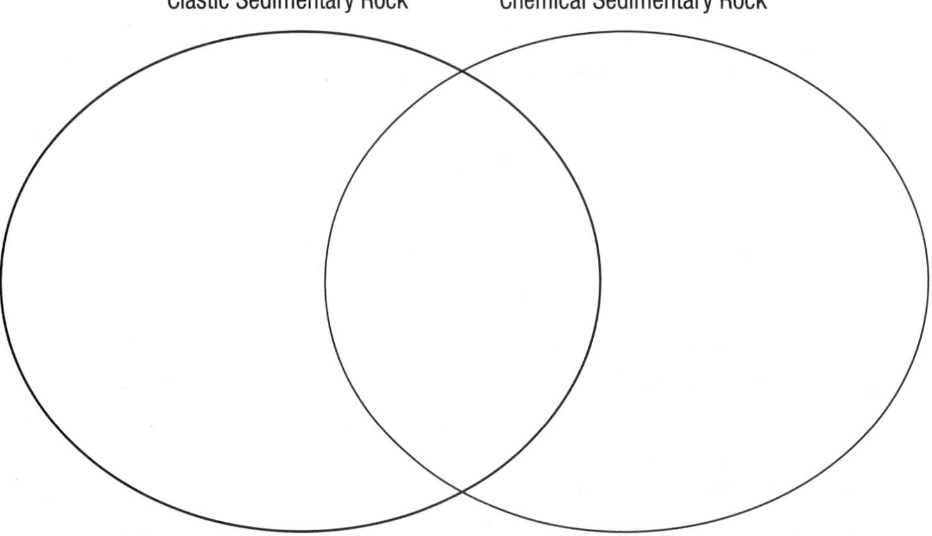

8. Circle the letters of the names of the rock groups that are classified as clastic sedimentary rocks.
   a. conglomerate
   b. breccia
   c. coquina
   d. sandstone

Features of Some Sedimentary Rocks

9. Is the following sentence true or false? In undisturbed sedimentary rocks, the oldest layers are found on the bottom. ________________

10. Ripple marks in a sedimentary rock may indicate that the rock formed along a(n) ________________ or ________________ bed.

11. What are the four major processes that form sedimentary rocks?

____

____

____

Name ______________________ Class ________________ Date ____________

Chapter 3 Rocks

Section 3.4 Metamorphic Rocks

This section discusses the formation and classification of metamorphic rocks.

Reading Strategy

Outlining This outline is a continuation of the outline from Section 3.3. Complete it as you read. Include points about how each of these rocks forms, some of the characteristics of each rock type, and some examples of each. For more information on this Reading Strategy, see the **Reading and Study Skills** in the **Skills and Reference Handbook** at the end of your textbook.

III. Metamorphic Rocks
- A. Foliated Rocks
  1. ______________________________
  2. ______________________________
- B. Nonfoliated Rocks
  1. ______________________________
  2. ______________________________

1. Is the following sentence true or false? Metamorphism means "a change in form." ______________

Formation of Metamorphic Rocks

Match each description to its term. The terms will be used more than once.

	Description	Term
_____	**2.** takes place when magma intrudes rock	a. contact metamorphism
_____	**3.** produces high-grade metamorphism	b. regional metamorphism
_____	**4.** produces low-grade metamorphism	
_____	**5.** changes in rock are minor	
_____	**6.** results in large-scale deformation	
_____	**7.** forms marble	
_____	**8.** occurs during mountain building	

Name ______________________ Class ________________ Date ____________

Chapter 3 Rocks

Agents of Metamorphism

9. The agents of metamorphism are ________________, ________________, and ________________ solutions.

10. Is the following sentence true or false? During metamorphism, rocks are usually subjected to one agent at a time.
____

11. Complete the table below.

Agents of Metamorphism	
Cause	**Effect**
Heat	
Pressure	
Reactions in solution	

Classification of Metamorphic Rocks

12. Circle the letter of each sentence that is true about foliated metamorphic rocks.
   a. It is rock with a layered or banded appearance.
   b. Pressure can form it.
   c. Gneiss and marble are examples of it.
   d. Schist is an example of it.

13. Circle the letter of each sentence that is true about nonfoliated metamorphic rocks.
   a. It is a metamorphic rock that does not have a banded texture.
   b. Most of it contains several different types of minerals.
   c. Marble is an example of it.
   d. Quartzite and anthracite are examples of it.

Name ______________ Class ______________ Date ______________

Section 4.1 Energy and Mineral Resources

This section discusses different types of resources, including renewable, nonrenewable, energy, and mineral resources.

Reading Strategy

Monitoring Your Understanding List what you know about energy and mineral resources in the first column and what you'd like to know in the second column. After you read, list what you have learned in the last column. For more information on this Reading Strategy, see the **Reading and Study Skills** in the **Skills and Reference Handbook** at the end of your textbook.

Energy and Mineral Resources		
What I Know	**What I Would Like to Know**	**What I Learned**
a.	c.	e.
b.	d.	f.

Renewable and Nonrenewable Resources

1. Is the following sentence true or false? Renewable resources can be replenished over fairly short time spans. ______________

2. A(n) ______________ resource takes millions of years to form and accumulate.

3. Circle the letter of the nonrenewable resource.
   - a. trees
   - b. sunlight
   - c. wind energy
   - d. natural gas

Fossil Fuels

4. What are three examples of fossil fuels? ______________

   ____

5. Circle the letter of the last stage of coal development.
   - a. anthracite
   - b. bituminous
   - c. lignite
   - d. peat

6. Is the following sentence true or false? Natural gas forms from the buried remains of animals and plants. ______________

Name ______________________ Class ______________________ Date ______________

Tar Sands and Oil Shale

Match each description with its fuel source.

	Description	Fuel Source
_____	7. World supplies are expected to dwindle in the future.	a. petroleum
_____	8. mixture of bitumen, water, clay, and sand	b. oil shale
_____	9. rock containing kerogen	c. tar sands

Formation of Mineral Deposits

10. Complete the table below.

Mineral Deposits		
Type	**How Forms**	**Mineral Examples**
Magma deposit		chromite, platinum
		gold, silver, mercury
	Eroded heavy minerals settle from moving water.	

Nonmetallic Mineral Resources

11. Circle the letter of the nonmetallic mineral resource.
   a. limestone
   b. gold
   c. chromite
   d. petroleum

12. Is the following sentence true or false? Nonmetallic mineral resources are used as a source of energy. ______________

Section 4.2 Alternate Energy Sources

This section discusses solar, nuclear, wind, hydroelectric, geothermal, and tidal energy.

Reading Strategy

Previewing Skim the section and complete the concept map for the various alternate energy sources. For more information on this Reading Strategy, see the **Reading and Study Skills** in the **Skills and Reference Handbook** at the end of your textbook.

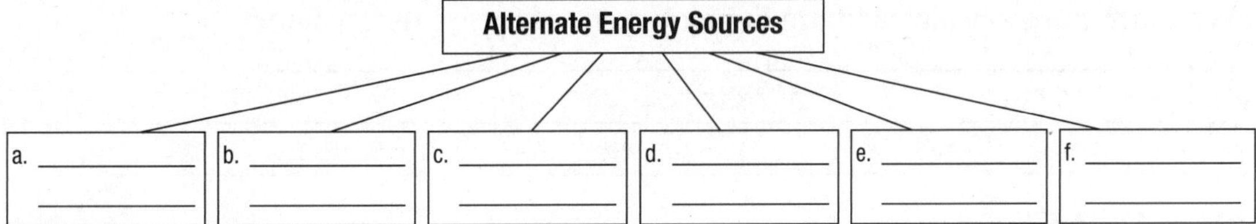

Solar Energy

1. What is solar energy? ____________

2. Complete the table below.

Solar Energy	
Advantages	**Disadvantages**
a.	a.
b.	b.

Nuclear Energy

3. Is the following sentence true or false? Uranium nuclei split during nuclear fission. ____________________

4. At a nuclear power plant, a nuclear chain reaction releases heat, which drives steam turbines that turn ____________________.

Wind Energy

5. Is the following sentence true or false? Experts estimate that 15 to 25 percent of the United States' electricity demand can be met by wind power in the next 50 to 60 years. ____________________

6. What are three obstacles to the development of future use of wind power? ____________________

Hydroelectric Power

7. What is hydroelectric power? ____________________

8. At a hydroelectric power plant, water is held in a(n) ____________________ behind a dam.

9. Circle the letter of the limiting factor in the development of hydroelectric power plants.
   a. limited water supplies
   b. noise pollution
   c. increase in cloudy days
   d. availability of suitable sites

Geothermal Energy

10. Circle the letter of the geothermal energy source that is used for heating and for turning turbines.
    a. hot water
    b. sunlight
    c. wind
    d. moving water

11. Is the following sentence true or false? The fuel used in geothermal energy is found above Earth's surface. ____________________

Tidal Power

12. Tidal power is harnessed by constructing a(n) ____________________ across the mouth of an estuary or a bay.

13. What drives the turbines and electric generators at a tidal power plant? ____________________

Name ______________________ Class ________________ Date __________

Section 4.3 Water, Air, and Land Resources

This section explains the importance of water, air, and land resources.

Reading Strategy

Building Vocabulary As you read, add definitions and examples to complete the table. For more information on this Reading Strategy, see the **Reading and Study Skills** in the **Skills and Reference Handbook** at the end of your textbook.

Definition	Example
point source pollution: pollution that can be traced to a location	factory pipes, sewer pipes
nonpoint source pollution: a.	b.
runoff: c.	d.
greenhouse gas: e.	f.

The Water Planet

1. List four ways people use fresh water. ____

____

____

Match each description with its term.

	Description	Term
_____	2. often carries nonpoint source pollution	a. runoff
_____	3. chemicals from a factory pipe	b. point source pollution
_____	4. pollution without a specific point of origin	c. nonpoint source pollution

Name ______________________ Class ______________ Date __________

Earth's Blanket of Air

5. The ______________ of Earth's atmosphere helps to maintain life on the planet.

6. Circle the letter of the gas in the atmosphere that people need to live.

   a. ozone b. oxygen
   c. water vapor d. nitrogen

7. What are gases such as carbon dioxide and methane called that help maintain the warm temperatures near the surface of Earth?

____

8. Fill in the blanks in the following flowchart.

Possible Effects of Global Warming

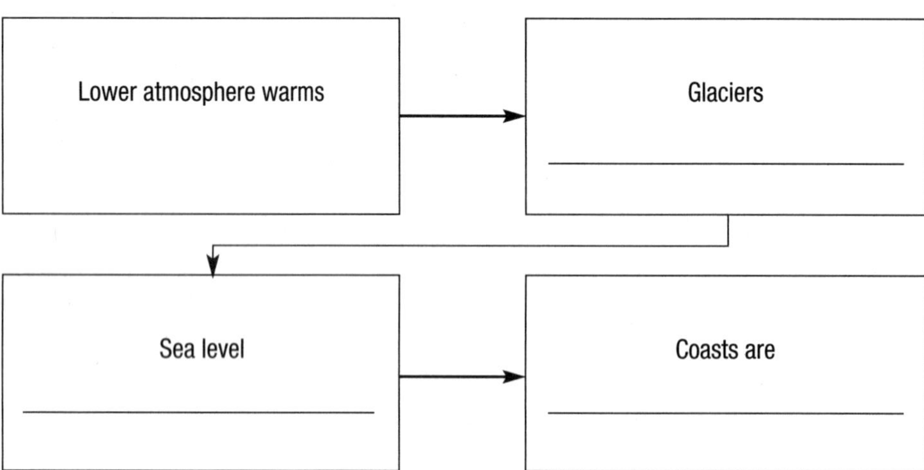

9. What is Earth's major source of air pollution?

____

Land Resources

10. List four resources that Earth's land provides.

____

____

____

11. Is the following sentence true or false? Agriculture has only a positive impact on the land. ______________

12. Is the following sentence true or false? Mineral mining can destroy vegetation and cause soil erosion. ______________

13. What negative impact can landfills have? ______________

____

____

____

Name ______________________ Class ________________ Date __________

Section 4.4 Protecting Resources

This section discusses laws passed to protect Earth's water, air, and land resources.

Reading Strategy

Summarizing After reading this section, complete the concept map to organize what you know about the major laws that help keep water, air, and land resources clean. For more information on this Reading Strategy, see the **Reading and Study Skills** in the **Skills and Reference Handbook** at the end of your textbook.

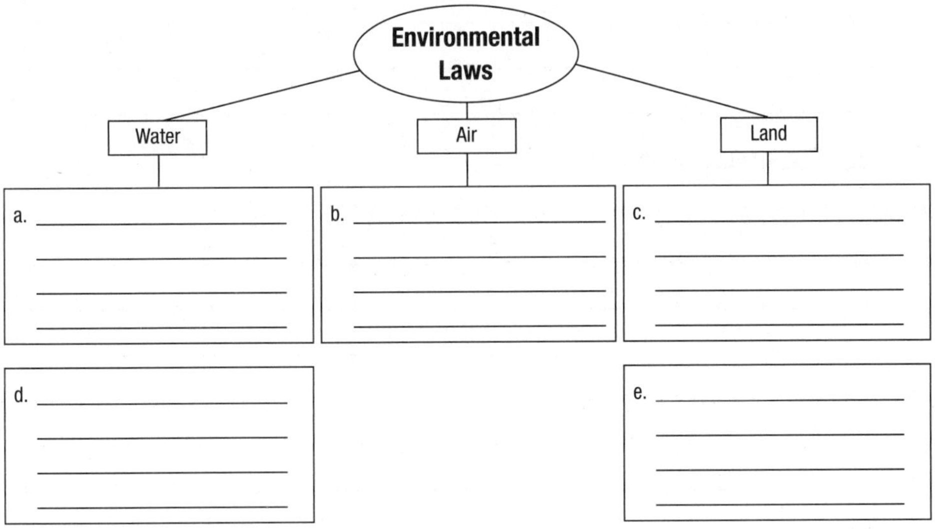

Environmental Laws

- Water
  - a. ______________________
  - d. ______________________
- Air
  - b. ______________________
- Land
  - c. ______________________
  - e. ______________________

Keeping Water Clean and Safe

1. Circle the letter of the term defined as "careful use of resources."
   a. recycling
   b. pollution
   c. composting
   d. conservation

2. Circle the letter of the law that requires industries to reduce or stop point source pollution into surface waters.
   a. Clean Air Act
   b. Safe Drinking Water Act
   c. Clean Water Act
   d. Resource Conservation and Recovery Act

3. Circle the letter of the law that sets maximum contaminant levels for water pollutants that could harm people's health.
   a. Clean Air Act
   b. Safe Drinking Water Act
   c. Clean Water Act
   d. Resource Conservation and Recovery Act

Name ______________ Class ______________ Date ______________

Protecting the Air

4. Is the following sentence true or false? The Clean Air Act is the United States' most important law for preventing air pollution.

____

5. How could using less electricity help to reduce air pollution?

____

____

____

____

____

____

____

Caring for Land Resources

6. What are two ways land resources can be protected?

____

____

____

____

____

____

Match each description with its term.

	Description	Term
_____	7. removing whole forest areas	a. recycling
_____	8. plowing across the contour of hillsides	b. selective cutting
_____	9. planting crops with different nutrient needs in adjacent rows	c. contour plowing
_____	10. fertilizer made of partly decomposed organic material	d. strip cropping
_____	11. Only some trees in a forest are cut.	e. compost
_____	12. collecting and processing used items to make new products	f. clear-cutting

13. What law requires companies to store, transport, and dispose of their hazardous wastes according to guidelines?

____

____

____

Name ______________________ Class __________________ Date ___________

Chapter 5 Weathering, Soil, and Mass Movements

Section 5.1 Weathering

This section describes different types of weathering in rocks.

Reading Strategy

Building Vocabulary As you read the section, define each vocabulary term. For more information on this Reading Strategy, see the **Reading and Study Skills** in the **Skills and Reference Handbook** at the end of your textbook.

Vocabulary Term	Definition
Mechanical weathering	a.
Frost wedging	b.
Talus	c.
Exfoliation	d.
Chemical weathering	e.

Mechanical Weathering

1. List and describe three types of mechanical weathering.

____

____

____

____

____

2. Is the following sentence true or false? In nature, three physical processes are especially important causes of mechanical weathering: chemical reactions, spheroidal weathering, and the presence of water. ______________

3. Circle the letter of each sentence that is true about mechanical weathering.
   a. Each piece of broken rock has the same characteristics as the original rock.
   b. In nature, three physical processes are especially important causes of mechanical weathering: frost wedging, unloading, and biological activity.
   c. When a rock is broken apart, less surface area is exposed to chemical weathering.
   d. Mechanical weathering is the transformation of rock into new compounds.

Chemical Weathering

4. Circle the letter of each sentence that is true about chemical weathering.

a. Water is the most important agent in chemical weathering.

b. Chemical weathering converts granite to clay minerals and quartz grains.

c. Chemical weathering can change the shape of a rock and its chemical composition.

d. Spheroidal weathering is a form of chemical weathering.

5. Describe the weathering process that the rocks in the photograph are undergoing.

____

____

6. The weathering process shown in the photograph is called ________________.

Rate of Weathering

7. Is the following sentence true or false? Factors that affect rate of weathering are surface area, rock characteristics, and climate. ________________

8. Two characteristics that affect rate of weathering are ________________ and ________________.

9. What are three ways that the climatic factors of temperature and moisture affect rate of weathering?

a. ______________________________

b. ______________________________

c. ______________________________

10. What are two factors that cause differential weathering?

____

____

Name ______________________ Class ________________ Date ___________

Section 5.2 Soil

This section describes the characteristics of soil.

Reading Strategy

Comparing and Contrasting As you read this section, compare the three types of soils by completing the table. For more information on this Reading Strategy, see the **Reading and Study Skills** in the **Skills and Reference Handbook** at the end of your textbook.

Soil Type	Where It's Found
Pedalfer	a.
Pedocal	b.
Laterite	c.

Characteristics of Soil

Match each description to its term.

Description

_____ **1.** layer of rock and mineral fragments

_____ **2.** part of the regolith that supports growth of plants

_____ **3.** decayed remains of organisms

Term

a. soil

b. humus

c. regolith

4. Is the following sentence true or false? Soil has four major components: mineral matter, humus, water, and air. ____________

5. Humus is a source of ________________, and it increases soil's ability to ________________.

6. Circle the letter of each sentence that is true about the functions that soil water serves in the soil.

a. Soil water provides the moisture needed for chemical reactions that sustain life.

b. Soil water is the source of carbon dioxide that plants use in photosynthesis.

c. Soil water provides nutrients in a form that plants can use.

d. All soils contain the same amount of soil water.

Soil Formation

7. The most important factors in soil formation are ________________, ________________, ________________, ________________, and ________________.

The Soil Profile

8. Write a brief description of each soil horizon on the figure below and label each of the soil horizons with the appropriate identifying letter.

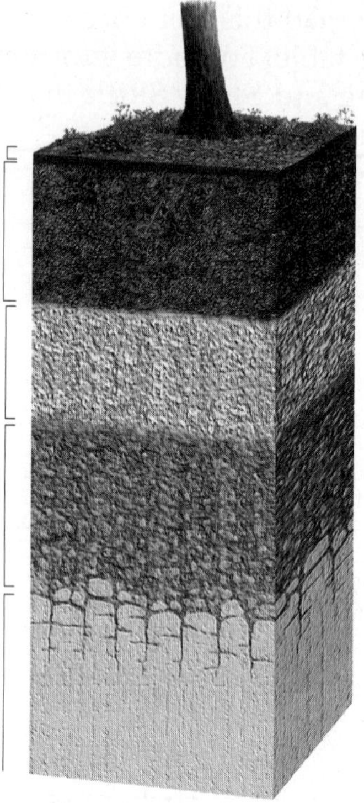

Soil Types

9. Write a brief description of each type of soil.

pedalfer ____

pedocal ____

laterite ____

10. Circle the letter of each sentence that is true about laterite.

a. Laterite is not a useful material for making bricks.

b. Laterite contains almost no organic matter.

c. Laterite is one of the poorest soils for agriculture.

d. In a newly cleared field, laterite can support agriculture for only a few years.

Soil Erosion

11. Is the following sentence true or false? Human activities, such as farming, logging, and construction, have slowed down the amount of erosion that occurs today. ________________

12. Is the following sentence true or false? In many regions of the world, soil is eroding faster than it is being formed.

____

Section 5.3 Mass Movements

This section describes situations in which large amounts of soil are moved naturally.

Reading Strategy

Previewing As you read the section, rewrite the green topic headings as *what* questions. Then write an answer to each question. For more information on this Reading Strategy, see the **Reading and Study Skills** in the **Skills and Reference Handbook** at the end of your textbook.

Question	Answer
a.	b.
c.	d.

1. The transfer of rock and soil downslope due to ______________ is called mass movement.

Triggers of Mass Movements

2. What are the factors that commonly trigger mass movements?

____

____

____

3. Circle the letter of each sentence that is true about water triggering mass movements.
   a. Heavy rains and rapid melting of snow can trigger mass movements by saturating surface materials with water.
   b. When the pores in sediment become filled with water, the particles slide past one another more easily.
   c. If there is sufficient water, sand grains will ooze downhill.
   d. Saturation of the ground with water makes slopes more susceptible to the force of gravity.

4. Is the following sentence true or false? If the steepness of a slope exceeds the stable angle, mass movements become more likely.

____

5. What are three possible causes of oversteepened slopes?

____

____

Types of Mass Movements

Match each description with its term.

	Description	Term
_____	**6.** a flow that moves relatively slowly—from about a millimeter per day to several meters per day	a. rockfall
_____	**7.** the downward movement of a block of material along a curved surface	b. rockslide
_____	**8.** a quickly moving mass of material that contains large amounts of water	c. slump
_____	**9.** when rock or rock fragments fall freely through the air	d. mudflow
_____	**10.** slides that include bedrock that move suddenly along a flat, inclined surface	e. earthflow

11. Identify each of the forms of mass wasting illustrated in the figures below by writing the name of the process on the lines provided. Choose *earthflow, slump,* or *rockslide.*

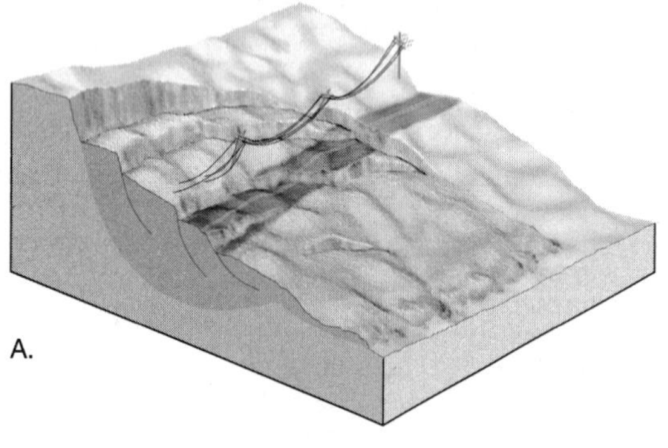

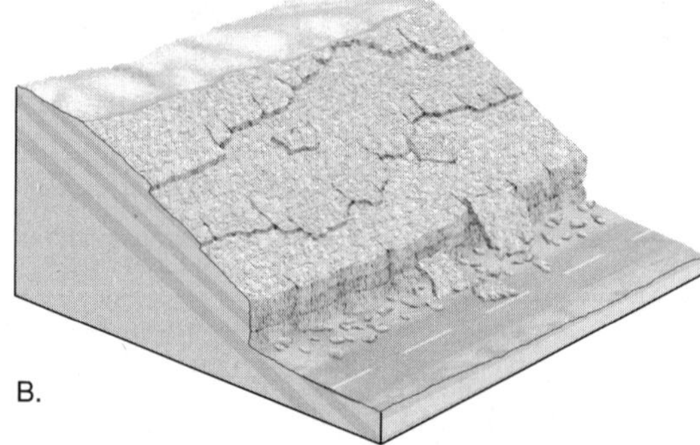

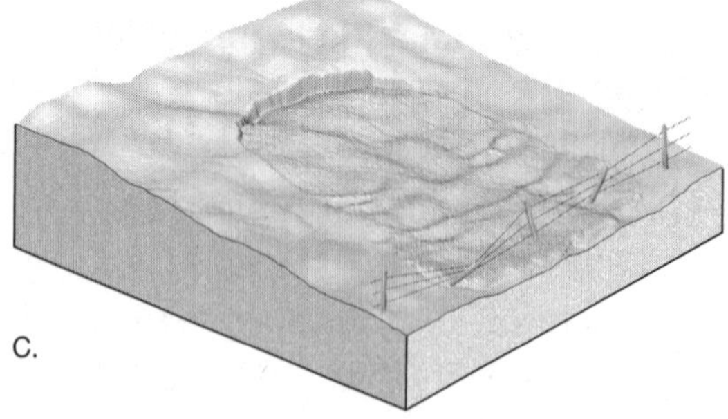

A. ____________________

B. ____________________

C. ____________________

Name ______________________ Class ______________ Date __________

Chapter 5 **Weathering, Soil, and Mass Movements**

WordWise

Test your knowledge of vocabulary terms from Chapter 5 by completing this crossword puzzle.

Clues across:

1. the part of the regolith that supports the growth of plants
6. soil usually found in drier western United States in areas that have grasses and brush vegetation
8. a layer of rock and mineral fragments produced by weathering
9. occurs when rocks or rock fragments fall freely through the air
11. the transfer of soil and rock downslope due to gravity
13. a vertical section through all of the soil horizons
15. downward movement of a block of material along a curved surface

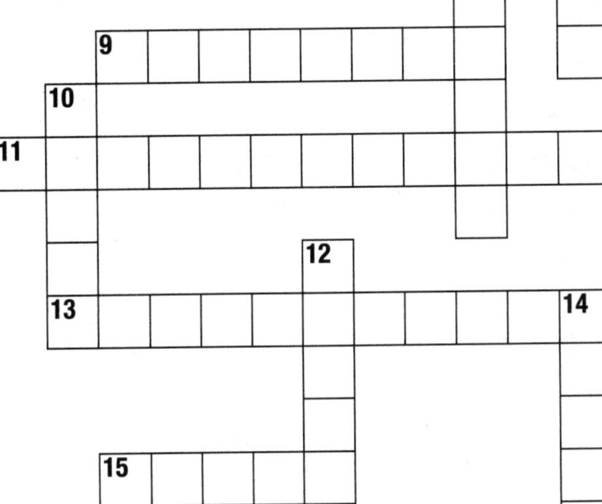

Clues down:

1. zones of soil that have similar composition, texture, structure, and color
2. flows that move quickly
3. a type of weathering in which physical forces break rock into smaller pieces without changing its composition
4. soil that forms in hot, wet tropical areas
5. flows that move relatively slowly
6. soil that usually forms in temperate areas
7. slides that include segments of bedrock
10. large piles of rock
12. the slowest type of mass movement
14. slabs of rock separating like layers of an onion

Name ______________________ Class ______________ Date __________

Section 6.1 Running Water

This section discusses the water cycle and how water flows in streams.

Reading Strategy

Building Vocabulary As you read this section, define in your own words each vocabulary term listed in the table. For more information on this Reading Strategy, see the **Reading and Study Skills** in the **Skills and Reference Handbook** at the end of your textbook.

Vocabulary Term	Definition
Water cycle	
Infiltration	
Transpiration	

The Water Cycle

1. Circle the letter of the term used to describe the unending circulation of Earth's water supply.

   a. water balance b. water cycle

   c. base level d. transpiration

2. Select the appropriate letter in the figure that represents each of the following processes in the water cycle.

   ______ runoff ______ evaporation

   ______ precipitation ______ infiltration

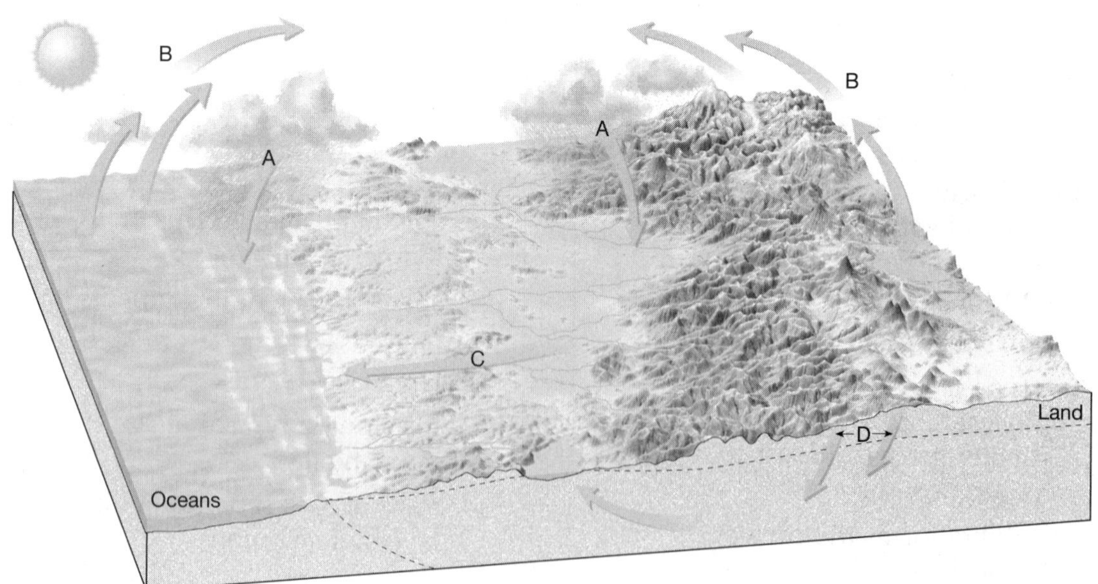

Earth's Water Balance

5. Earth's water cycle is balanced in that each year the average amount of precipitation that occurs over Earth is equal to the amount of water that ________________.

Streamflow

6. A stream's ability to pick up and move material depends largely on its ________________.
7. What are five factors that determine the velocity of a stream?

____

____

____

Match each definition with its term.

	Definition	Term
_____	8. course that water in a stream follows	a. gradient
_____	9. volume of water flowing past a certain point in a given unit of time	b. discharge
_____	10. steepness of a stream channel	c. velocity
_____	11. distance that water travels in a period of time	d. stream channel

Changes from Upstream to Downstream

12. Is the following sentence true or false? A stream's discharge increases between the headwaters and mouth of the stream.

____

13. Is the following sentence true or false? From its headwaters to its mouth, a stream's gradient increases. ________________

Base Level

14. Circle the letter of the lowest point to which a stream can erode its channel.
    a. mouth
    b. headwaters
    c. valley
    d. base level
15. Circle the letter of what a bend in a stream is called.
    a. meander
    b. tributary
    c. mouth
    d. valley

Name ______________________ Class ________________ Date ____________

Section 6.2 The Work of Streams

This section discusses streams and explains how they help shape Earth's surface.

Reading Strategy

Comparing and Contrasting Preview the Key Concepts, topic headings, vocabulary, and figures in this section. List things you expect to learn about each. After reading, state what you learned about each item you listed. For more information on this Reading Strategy, see the **Reading and Study Skills** in the **Skills and Reference Handbook** at the end of your textbook.

What I Expect to Learn	What I Learned

Erosion

1. How do streams erode their channels?

____

____

Sediment Transport

2. Circle the letter of the name for the material a stream carries in solution.
   a. bed load
   b. suspended load
   c. dissolved load
   d. mineral load
3. Circle the letter of what the large, solid material a stream carries along its bed is called.
   a. bed load
   b. suspended load
   c. dissolved load
   d. maximum load
4. Is the following sentence true or false? As a stream's velocity decreases, its competence increases. ________________
5. A stream's ________________ is the maximum load it can carry.
6. Is the following sentence true or false? Most streams carry the largest part of their load in suspension. ________________

Name ______________________ Class ______________ Date ___________

Deposition

7. When stream flow decreases to below the critical settling velocity of a certain size particle, ________________ occurs.

8. How does a delta form? ____

____

9. Circle the letter that represents natural levees in the figure below.

a. A   b. B   c. C   d. D

Stream Valleys

10. Circle the letter that represents an oxbow lake in the figure above.

a. A   b. B   c. C   d. D

11. What shape will a stream valley have if its primary work has been downward erosion cutting toward base level?

____

12. A stream's ________________ is the flat valley floor onto which it overflows its banks during flooding.

Floods and Flood Control

Match each description with its term.

	Description	Term
_____	13. earthen mounds built on river banks	a. artificial levees
_____	14. structures that store floodwater and let it out slowly	b. floods
_____	15. mostly caused by rapid snowmelt and storms	c. flood-control dams

Drainage Basins

16. A(n) ________________ is an imaginary line separating different drainage basins.

17. The land area that contributes water to a stream is known as a(n) ________________.

Name ______________________ Class ________________ Date ____________

Section 6.3 Water Beneath the Surface

This section discusses groundwater, including the environmental threats posed to it and landforms associated with it.

Reading Strategy

Comparing and Contrasting Before you read the section, rewrite the green topic headings as *how, why,* and *what* questions. As you read, write an answer to each question. For more information on this Reading Strategy, see the **Reading and Study Skills** in the **Skills and Reference Handbook** at the end of your textbook.

Question	Answer
How does water move underground?	

Distribution and Movement of Water Underground

1. Select the appropriate letter in the figure that identifies each of the following groundwater features.

_____ zone of saturation

_____ aquitard

_____ spring

_____ water table

_____ zone of aeration

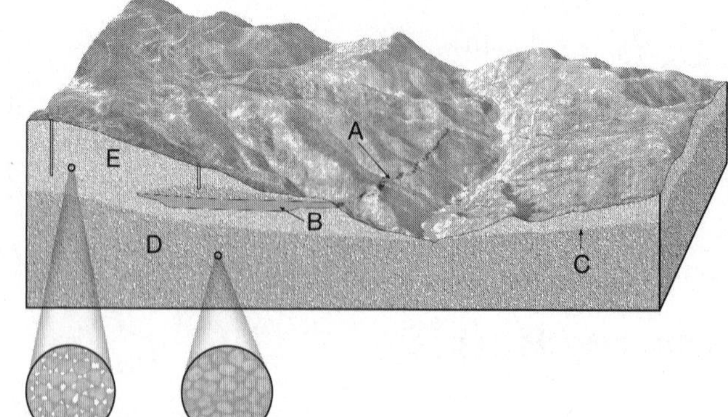

2. Is the following sentence true or false? Groundwater moves faster through sediment with large pore spaces than through sediment with small pore spaces.

____

Name ______________________ Class ________________ Date ____________

Springs

3. Circle the letter of the following that forms whenever the ground surface and water table intersect.

a. aquifer
b. spring
c. well
d. aquitard

4. A type of spring called a(n) ________________ is a column of water that shoots up intermittently with great force.

Wells

5. Circle the letter of the location a well must be drilled to provide a continuous water supply.

a. in the zone of aeration
b. far below the water table
c above the zone of saturation
d. far above the water table

6. What two conditions must exist for an artesian well to form? ________________

____

____

____

Environmental Problems Associated with Groundwater

7. What are two things that threaten groundwater supplies?

____

Caverns

Match each description with its groundwater feature .

	Description	Groundwater Feature
_____	**8.** dripstone feature that forms on a cavern ceiling	a. cavern
_____	**9.** type of limestone deposited in caverns by dripping water	b. travertine
_____	**10.** natural process that forms caverns	c. stalactite
_____	**11.** naturally formed underground chamber	d. stalagmite
_____	**12.** dripstone feature that forms on a cavern floor	e. erosion

Karst Topography

13. Typical of karst areas are depressions called ________________.

14. Is the following sentence true or false? Areas with karst topography typically have irregular terrain. ________________

Name ______________________ Class ________________ Date __________

WordWise

Use the clues below to identify vocabulary terms from Chapter 6. Write the terms, putting one letter in each blank. Use the circled letters to find the hidden word.

Clues

1. how plants release water into the atmosphere

2. a stream's slope

3. the movement of surface water into rock or soil through cracks and pore spaces

4. a sediment's ability to release a fluid

5. a permeable rock layer that transmits groundwater freely

6. a triangular shaped sediment accumulation

7. the maximum load a stream can carry

8. the water within the zone of saturation

9. the percentage of a rock that is occupied by pore spaces

Vocabulary Terms

1. _ _ _ _ _ _ _ _ _ ◯ _ _ _
2. _ ◯ _ _ _ _ _ _
3. ◯ _ _ _ _ _ _ _ _ _ _ _
4. _ _ _ _ _ _ ◯ _ _ _ _ _
5. _ _ ◯ _ _ _ _
6. _ _ _ ◯ _
7. _ _ _ ◯ _ _ _ _
8. _ ◯ _ _ _ _ _ _ _ _ _
9. _ _ _ _ _ _ _ ◯

Hidden Word: _ _ _ _ _ _ _ _ _

Definition: ____

____

Section 7.1 Glaciers

This section discusses the characteristics of different types of glaciers.

Reading Strategy

Building Vocabulary As you read this section, define each vocabulary term in your own words. For more information on this Reading Strategy, see the **Reading and Study Skills** in the **Skills and Reference Handbook** at the end of your textbook.

Vocabulary Term	Definition
Ice age	a.
Glacier	b.
Snowline	c.
Valley glacier	d.
Ice sheet	e.
Glacial trough	f.
Till	g.
Stratified drift	h.
Moraine	i.

Types of Glaciers

1. A __________________ is a stream of ice that flows between steep rock walls from a place near the top of a mountain valley.
2. __________________ cover large regions where the climate is extremely cold.

How Glaciers Move

3. Circle the letter of each sentence that is true about how glaciers move.
   a. Glacial flow happens in two ways: plastic flow and basal slip.
   b. All glaciers move at about the same speed.
   c. The movement of a glacier depends upon the balance between accumulation and wastage.
   d. Basal slip occurs because of gravity.

Name ______________________ Class ________________ Date __________

Glacial Erosion

4. Name and describe the two types of glacial erosion.

____

____

____

Landforms Created by Glacial Erosion

5. The area shown in the figure was subjected to alpine glaciation. Select the appropriate letter in the figure that identifies each of the following features.

_____ cirque
_____ glacial trough
_____ hanging valley
_____ horn
_____ arête

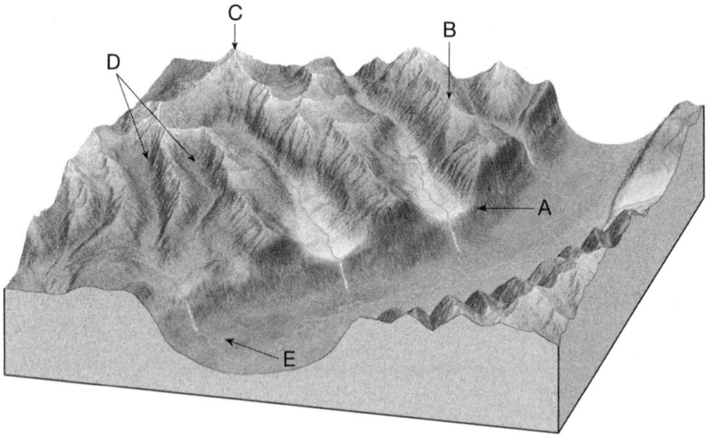

Glacial Deposits

6. ________________ applies to all sediments of glacial origin, no matter how, where, or in what form they were deposited.

7. The two types of glacial drift are ________________ and ________________.

Moraines, Outwash Plains, and Kettles

Match each description to its term.

	Description	Term
_____	**8.** layers or ridges of till	a. end moraine
_____	**9.** debris that forms at the end of a stationary glacier	b. kettle
_____	**10.** debris that forms by a receding glacier	c. moraine
_____	**11.** formed when blocks of stagnant ice become buried in drift	d. ground moraine

Glaciers of the Ice Age

12. Is the following sentence true or false? During the recent ice age, the Northern Hemisphere had twice the ice of the Southern Hemisphere. ________________

Name ______________________ Class ________________ Date __________

Section 7.2 Deserts

This section explains the weathering and erosion processes that occur in the desert.

Reading Strategy

Summarizing As you read this section, write a brief summary of the text for each blue heading. For more information on this Reading Strategy, see the **Reading and Study Skills** in the **Skills and Reference Handbook** at the end of your textbook.

Weathering
____
____
____
The Role of Water
____
____
____

Weathering in Deserts

1. Much of the weathered debris in deserts is a result of ________________.

2. Why is rock weathering of any type greatly reduced in a desert climate? ______________________________

3. Circle the letter of each sentence that is true about weathering and desert landscapes.
   a. Most weathering debris that is formed consists of rocks and minerals that are chemically unchanged.
   b. The rust-colored tint of some desert landscapes is due to iron-bearing silicate materials.
   c. Most of the weathering in desert climates is due to chemical weathering.
   d. Large amounts of organic acids that are present in the landscape cause a great deal of chemical weathering.

Water in Deserts

4. Explain why desert climates often have streams.

____

____

____

Match each description to its term.

	Description	Term
_____	**5.** streams that carry water only after it rains	a. alluvial fan
_____	**6.** sediment that is carried down mountain canyons and deposited on the gentle slopes at the base of the mountains	b. playa lake
_____	**7.** formed when an alluvial fan receives abundant rainfall	c. running water
_____	**8.** the source of most desert erosion	d. desert streams

9. Complete the following concept map.

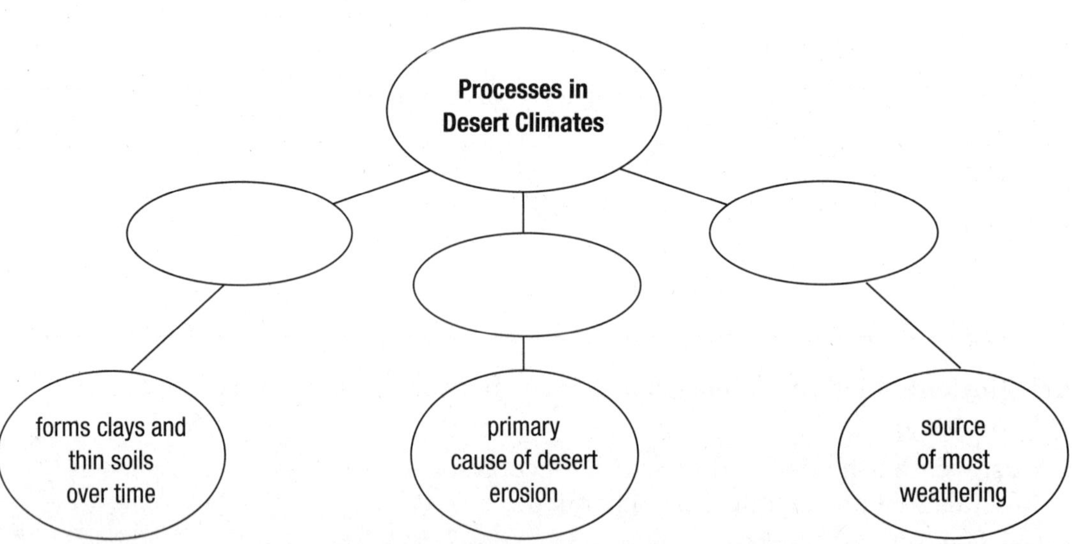

10. Circle the letter of each sentence that is true about a desert landscape.
    a. Arid regions typically have interior drainage.
    b. A dry, flat lakebed that was formerly a playa lake is called a playa.
    c. The Nile River is an example of a permanent stream that crosses an arid region.
    d. The Colorado River is a desert stream.
11. Is the following sentence true or false? Arid regions have complex systems of rivers and streams that drain excess water from the region into oceans. ________________

Name ______________________ Class ________________ Date ____________

Section 7.3 Landscapes Shaped by Wind

This section describes how winds shape various landforms.

Reading Strategy

Outlining As you read, make an outline of this section. Use the green headings as the main topics and the blue headings as subtopics. Add supporting details to the outline. For more information on this Reading Strategy, see the **Reading and Study Skills** in the **Skills and Reference Handbook** at the end of your textbook.

Landscapes Shaped by Wind
I. Wind Erosion
A. Deflation
B. Abrasion
II. ______________________
A. ______________________
B. ______________________
III. ______________________
A. ______________________
B. ______________________
C. ______________________
D. ______________________
E. ______________________
F. ______________________

Wind Erosion

Match each description to its term.

	Description	Term
_____	**1.** shallow depressions caused by deflation	a. deflation
_____	**2.** a stony surface caused by deflation	b. abrasion
_____	**3.** the cutting and polishing of exposed rock surfaces by windblown sand	c. blowouts
_____	**4.** the lifting and removal of loose particles such as clay and silt	d. desert pavement

5. Circle the letter of each statement that is true about wind erosion.
   a. Wind is the source of more erosion than water, even in desert climates.
   b. Wind erodes the desert in two ways: deflation and abrasion.
   c. All blowouts caused by deflation are about the same size.
   d. Sand rarely travels more than a meter above the surface, so the wind's sandblasting effect is limited in the vertical direction.

Wind Deposits

6. Is the following sentence true or false? Layers of loess and sand dunes are landscaping features deposited by water.
   ____

7. ____________________ is windblown silt that blankets the landscape.

8. Circle the letter of each statement that is true about wind deposits.
   a. The thickest and most extensive deposits of loess on Earth occur in western and northern China.
   b. Significant loess deposits are found in portions of South Dakota, Nebraska, Iowa, Missouri, Illinois, and the Pacific Northwest.
   c. Winds commonly deposit sand in mounds or ridges called dunes.
   d. Dunes occur on unobstructed flat ground.

Types of Sand Dunes

9. Write the type of each dune illustrated in the figures below.

   A. ____________________
   B. ____________________
   C. ____________________
   D. ____________________

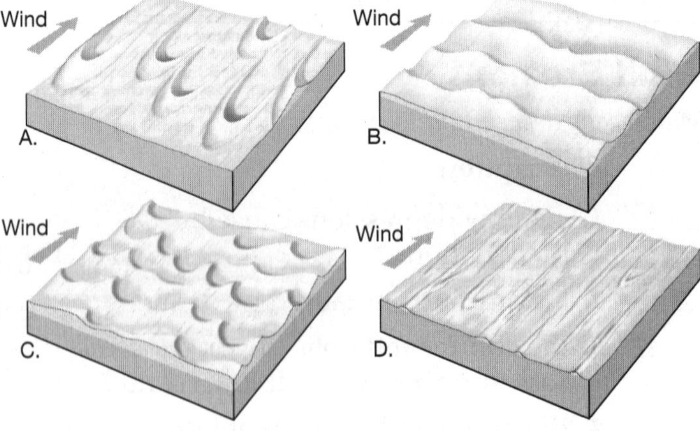

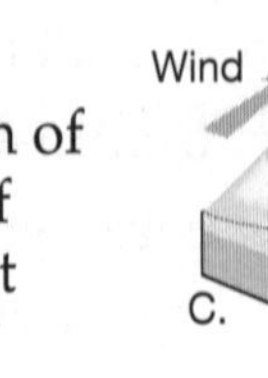

10. Give a brief description of two additional types of sand dunes that are not shown in the figure.
    ____
    ____
    ____
    ____
    ____
    ____

Name ______________________ Class ________________ Date ____________

Section 8.1 What Is an Earthquake?

This section explains what earthquakes and faults are and what causes earthquakes.

Reading Strategy

Building Vocabulary As you read this section, write a definition for each vocabulary term in your own words. For more information on this Reading Strategy, see the **Reading and Study Skills** in the **Skills and Reference Handbook** at the end of your textbook.

Vocabulary	Definition
earthquake	a.
fault	b.
focus	c.
epicenter	d.

1. Circle the letter of the approximate number of major earthquakes that take place each year.
   a. about 50 b. about 75
   c. about 3000 d. about 30,000

Earthquakes

Match each description with its earthquake feature.

Description

_____ 2. Earth vibration caused by rapid energy release

_____ 3. energy that radiates in all directions from the earthquake origin

_____ 4. fracture where movement has occurred

_____ 5. surface location directly above where an earthquake originates

_____ 6. location within Earth where an earthquake originates

Earthquake Feature

a. epicenter
b. focus
c. seismic wave
d. fault
e. earthquake

Name ______________________ Class ________________ Date ____________

The Cause of Earthquakes

7. Is the following sentence true or false? It was not until after the 1906 San Francisco earthquake was studied that the actual cause of earthquakes was understood. ________________

8. Complete the flowchart to show the sequence of events that occur when rocks are deformed along a fault.

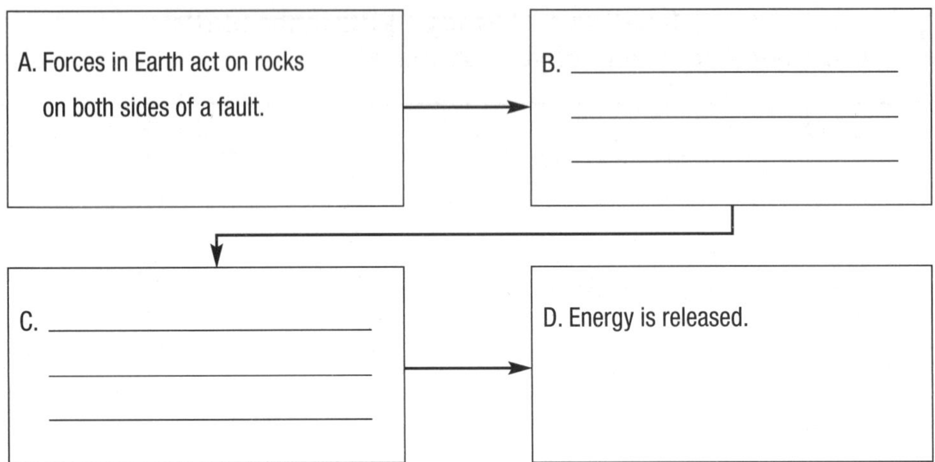

9. The ________________ hypothesis states that when rocks are deformed, they bend and then break, releasing stored energy.

10. What causes most earthquakes? ________________

11. Is the following sentence true or false? Most earthquakes occur along existing faults. ________________

12. Circle the letter of small Earth movements that occur following a major earthquake.
    a. foreshocks
    b. slippage
    c. aftershocks
    d. foci

13. The ________________ is one of the most studied fault systems in the world.

14. What is fault creep? ________________

Name ______________________ Class ________________ Date __________

Section 8.2 Measuring Earthquakes

This section discusses types of seismic waves and how earthquakes are located and measured.

Reading Strategy

Outlining As you read, fill in the outline with the important ideas in this section. Use the green headings as the main topics and the blue headings as subtopics. For more information on this Reading Strategy, see the **Reading and Study Skills** in the **Skills and Reference Handbook** at the end of your textbook

Measuring Earthquakes
I. Seismic Waves
A. Body Waves
B. ______________
C. ______________
II. ______________
A. ______________
B. ______________
III. ______________
A. ______________
B. ______________
C. ______________
IV. ______________

Recording Seismic Waves

1. Circle the letter of the type of seismic wave that shakes particles at right angles to their direction of travel.
   a. P waves
   b. S waves
   c. surface waves
   d. compression waves

2. The figure shows a typical recording of an earthquake. Select the appropriate letter in the figure that identifies each of the following types of seismic waves.

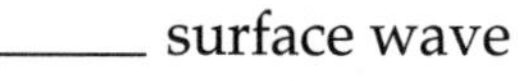

______ surface wave

______ S wave

______ P wave

3. Circle the letter of the name of the recording of the three types of seismic waves in the figure on page 57.

a. seismograph b. seismogram

c. seismic wave d. travel-time graph

Measuring Earthquakes

4. What two types of measurements do scientists use to describe the size of earthquakes? ______________________

Match each description with its term related to earthquake measurement.

	Description	Term
____	**5.** derived from the amount of displacement that occurs along a fault zone	a. intensity
____	**6.** based on the amplitude of the largest seismic wave recorded on a seismogram	b. magnitude
____	**7.** measure of the size of seismic waves or amount of energy released at the earthquake source	c. Richter scale
____	**8.** measure of the amount of earthquake shaking at a location based on damage	d. moment magnitude scale

9. What measurement do scientists today use for earthquakes?

____

10. Why is the answer to question 9 the most widely used measurement for earthquakes? ______________________

____

____

____

Locating an Earthquake

11. Is the following sentence true or false? On a seismogram, the greater the interval is between the arrival of the first P wave and the first S wave, the greater the distance to the earthquake source.

____

12. Is the following sentence true or false? You can use travel-time graphs from two seismographs to find the exact location of an earthquake epicenter. ______________

Name ______________________ Class __________________ Date ____________

Section 8.3 Earthquake Hazards

This section discusses damage caused by earthquakes and explains how earthquakes are predicted.

Reading Strategy

Monitoring Your Understanding Preview the Key Concepts, topic headings, vocabulary, and figures in this section. List two things you expect to learn. After reading, state what you learned about each item you listed. For more information on this Reading Strategy, see the **Reading and Study Skills** in the **Skills and Reference Handbook** at the end of your textbook.

What I Expect to Learn	What I Learned
a.	b.
c.	d.

Causes of Earthquake Damage

1. What risk does liquefaction pose during an earthquake?

____

____

2. Is the following sentence true or false? Most earthquakes generate tsunamis. ________________

3. The sinking of the ground caused by earthquake vibrations is called ground ________________.

4. During an earthquake, violent shaking can cause soil and rock on slopes to move, resulting in ________________.

5. Complete the table about tsunamis.

Tsunamis		
Definition	**Causes**	**Areas Protected from Tsunamis by Warning System**
	a. b.	

Reducing Earthquake Damage

6. List three factors that affect the degree of damage that occurs to structures as a result of earthquakes.

____

____

____

7. Circle the letter of the structure that is least likely to be damaged in a major earthquake.
   a. reinforced steel-frame building
   b. nonflexible wood-frame building
   c. unreinforced stone building
   d.unreinforced brick building

8. Is the following sentence true or false? Methods used to make short-range earthquake predictions have not been successful.
   ____

9. Is the following sentence true or false? Scientists are able to make accurate long-term earthquake predictions based on their understanding of how earthquakes occur. ____________________

10. What do scientists call an area along a fault where no earthquake activity has occurred for a long time? ____________________

This section describes Earth's layers and their composition.

Reading Strategy

Sequencing After you read, complete the sequence of layers in Earth's interior. For more information on this Reading Strategy, see the **Reading and Study Skills** in the **Skills and Reference Handbook** at the end of your textbook.

Earth's Internal Structure

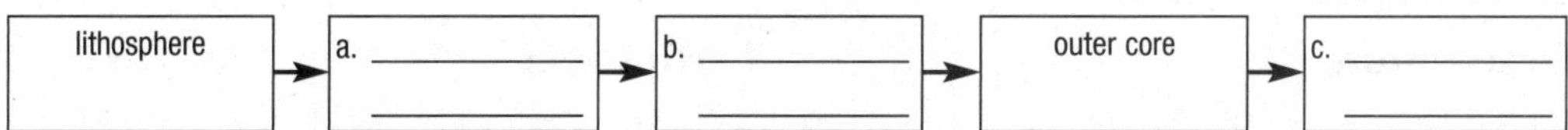

Layers Defined by Composition

1. Use the figure of Earth's structure to write the letter(s) that represents each of the following layers.

   mantle ______________

   continental crust ______________

   oceanic crust ______________

   core ______________

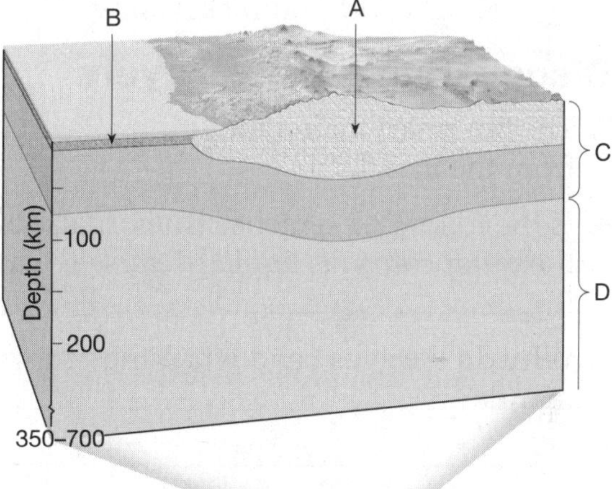

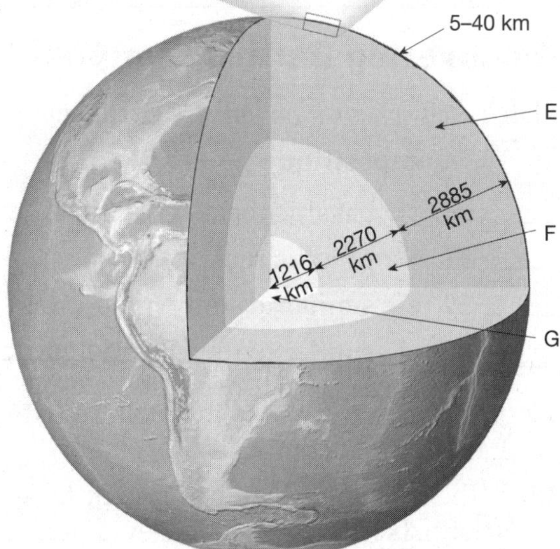

Name ____________________ Class ____________________ Date ____________

Layers Defined by Physical Properties

2. Use the figure of Earth's structure on the previous page to write the letter that represents each of the following layers.

inner core ____________________

asthenosphere ____________________

outer core ____________________

lithosphere ____________________

Match each description with its Earth layer.

	Description	**Earth Layer**
_____	**3.** soft, weak rock near its melting point	a. asthenosphere
_____	**4.** liquid iron-nickel alloy that generates Earth's magnetic field	b. inner core
_____	**5.** cool, rigid crust and uppermost mantle	c. outer core
_____	**6.** solid iron-nickel alloy	d. lithosphere

Discovering Earth's Layers

7. The boundary called the ____________________ separates the crust from the mantle.

8. Is the following sentence true or false? Geologists concluded that the outer core was liquid because P waves could not travel through it. ____________________

9. Why do P waves bend when they travel into the outer core from the mantle? ____________________

____

____

Discovering Earth's Composition

Match each composition with its Earth layer.

	Composition	**Earth Layer**
_____	**10.** basaltic rock	a. continental crust
_____	**11.** granitic rock	b. oceanic crust
_____	**12.** similar to stony meteorites	c. core
_____	**13.** similar to metallic meteorites	d. mantle

14. ____________________ that collide with Earth provide evidence of Earth's inner composition.

15. Is the following sentence true or false? Until the late 1960s, scientists had only seismic evidence they could use to determine the composition of oceanic crust. ____________________

Name _______________ Class _______________ Date _______________

Section 9.1 Continental Drift

This section explains the hypothesis of continental drift and the evidence supporting it.

Reading Strategy

Summarizing Fill in the table as you read to summarize the evidence of continental drift. For more information on this Reading Strategy, see the **Reading and Study Skills** in the **Skills and Reference Handbook** at the end of your textbook.

Hypothesis	Evidence
Continental Drift	a. continental puzzle
	b.
	c.
	d.

The Continental Puzzle

1. Wegener called Earth's ancient supercontinent _______________.

Evidence for Continental Drift

Match each example of continental drift with the type of evidence it is.

Example

_____ 2. Similar mountain chains run through eastern North America and the British Isles.

_____ 3. Land areas that show evidence of ancient glaciation are now located near the equator.

_____ 4. The Atlantic coastlines of South America and Africa fit together.

_____ 5. Remains of *Mesosaurus* are limited to eastern South America and southern Africa.

Evidence for Continental Drift

a. rock types and structures

b. matching fossils

c. continental puzzle

d. ancient climates

6. _______________ evidence for continental drift includes several fossil organisms found on different landmasses.

7. Is the following sentence true or false? If the continents existed as Pangaea, the rocks found in a particular region on one continent should closely match in age and type those in adjacent positions on the adjoining continent. _______________

8. The figure shows Earth's ancient supercontinent as it appeared about 300 million years ago, according to Alfred Wegener. Write the letter that represents each of the following present-day continents.

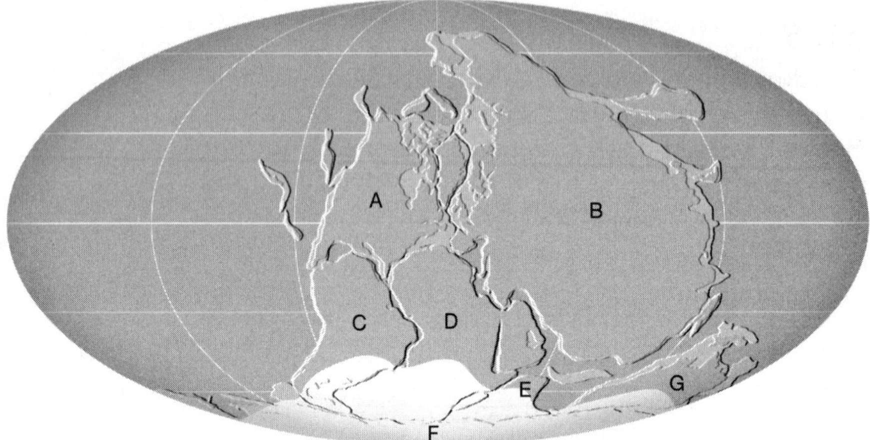

_____ Antarctica
_____ Europe and Asia
_____ South America
_____ India
_____ North America
_____ Africa
_____ Australia

Rejection of Wegener's Hypothesis

9. Circle the letter of an example of one objection that critics had about Wegener's continental drift hypothesis.
   a. Wegener could not provide any evidence to support continental drift.
   b. Wegener could not propose a mechanism capable of moving the continents.
   c. Wegener's idea of the mechanism capable of moving the continents was physically impossible.
   d. Wegener's fossil evidence was not accurate.

10. Is the following sentence true or false? Most scientists in Wegener's time supported his continental drift hypothesis.
   ____

11. Is the following sentence true or false? Wegener proposed that during continental drift, larger continents broke through the oceanic crust. ____________________

12. By 1968, data collected about the ocean floor, earthquake activity, and the magnetic field led to a new theory called ____________________.

13. The new theory that replaced Wegener's hypothesis explained most geologic processes, including the formation of ____________________.

Name ______________________ Class ________________ Date ___________

Section 9.2 Sea-Floor Spreading

This section discusses sea-floor spreading and subduction zones, and evidence for sea-floor spreading.

Reading Strategy

Identifying Supporting Evidence Copy the graphic organizer. After you read, complete it to show the types of evidence that supported the hypothesis of sea-floor spreading. For more information on this Reading Strategy, see the **Reading and Study Skills** in the **Skills and Reference Handbook** at the end of your textbook.

Evidence	Hypothesis
a. ______________________	
b. ______________________	sea-floor spreading
c. ______________________	

Exploring the Ocean Floor

Match each definition with its term.

	Definition	Term
_____	**1.** system that uses sound waves to calculate the distance to an object	a. sonar
_____	**2.** deep faulted structure found along a divergent boundary	b. rift valley
_____	**3.** elevated seafloor along a divergent boundary	c. oceanic ridge

The Process of Sea-Floor Spreading

4. Circle the letter of the description of a subduction zone.

a. where an oceanic plate is forced beneath a second plate

b. where an oceanic plate grinds past a second plate

c. where a continental plate grinds past a second plate

d. where an oceanic plate moves away from a second plate

Evidence for Sea-Floor Spreading

5. ________________ has occurred when rocks formed millions of years ago show the location of the magnetic poles at the time of their formation.

6. Is the following sentence true or false? When magnetic mineral grains in a rock form, they become magnetized in the direction parallel to Earth's existing magnetic field. ________________

7. Circle the letter of the statement representing some of the strongest evidence of sea-floor spreading.
   a. Similar fossils are found in North America and Europe.
   b. Earth's magnetic field periodically reverses polarity.
   c. Strips of alternating polarity lie as mirror images across the ocean ridges.
   d. Evidence of glaciation occurs on land in tropical and subtropical regions.

8. Circle the letter of the definition of reverse polarity.
   a. the loss of magnetism by iron-rich mineral grains when heated
   b. the gain of magnetism by iron-rich mineral grains when cooled
   c. what rocks that show the same magnetism as the present magnetic field have
   d. what rocks that show the opposite magnetism as the present magnetic field have

9. Is the following sentence true or false? Deep-focus earthquakes occur away from ocean trenches within the slab of lithosphere descending into the mantle. ________________

10. Where do shallow-focus earthquakes occur relative to ocean trenches? ____

    ____

11. Circle the letter of the location of the oldest oceanic crust, according to ocean drilling data.
    a. near the edges of continents
    b. at the ridge crest
    c. between the continental margins and ridge crest
    d. deep in the asthenosphere

12. Circle the letter of the location of the youngest oceanic crust, according to ocean drilling data.
    a. at the continental margins
    b. at the ridge crest
    c. between the continental margins and ridge crest
    d. deep in the asthenosphere

Name ______________________ Class ________________ Date ___________

Section 9.3 Theory of Plate Tectonics

This section discusses plate tectonics, including lithospheric plates and types of plate boundaries.

Reading Strategy

Comparing and Contrasting After you read, compare the three types of plate boundaries by completing the table. For more information on this Reading Strategy, see the **Reading and Study Skills** in the **Skills and Reference Handbook** at the end of your textbook.

Boundary Type	Relative Plate Motion
convergent	a.
divergent	b.
transform fault	c.

Earth's Moving Plates

1. Is the following sentence true or false? The lithospheric plates move at about 5 km per year. ________________

2. Identify each type of plate boundary shown in the figure.

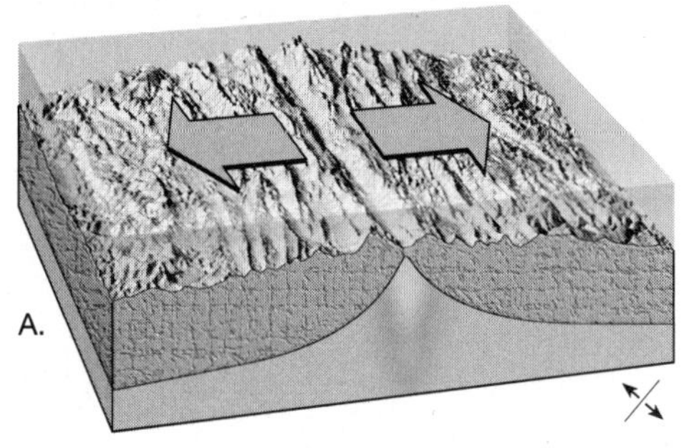

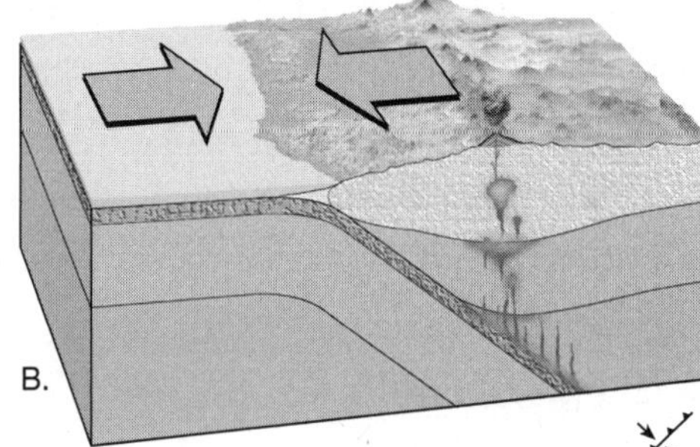

A. ____________________

B. ____________________

C. ____________________

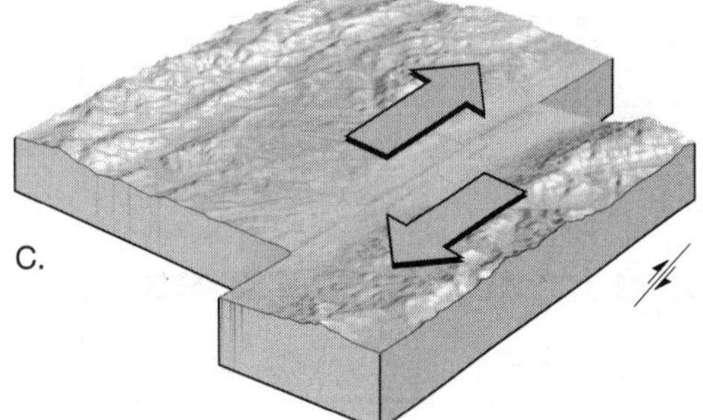

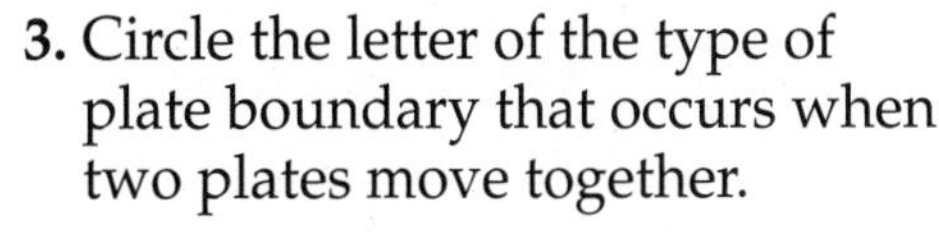

3. Circle the letter of the type of plate boundary that occurs when two plates move together.
   a. divergent
   b. spreading center
   c. convergent
   d. transform fault

Divergent Boundaries

4. Is the following sentence true or false? Oceanic lithosphere is created at divergent boundaries. ________________

5. Is the following sentence true or false? Divergent boundaries only occur on the ocean floor. ________________

Convergent Boundaries

6. Select the appropriate letter in the figure that identifies each of the following features.

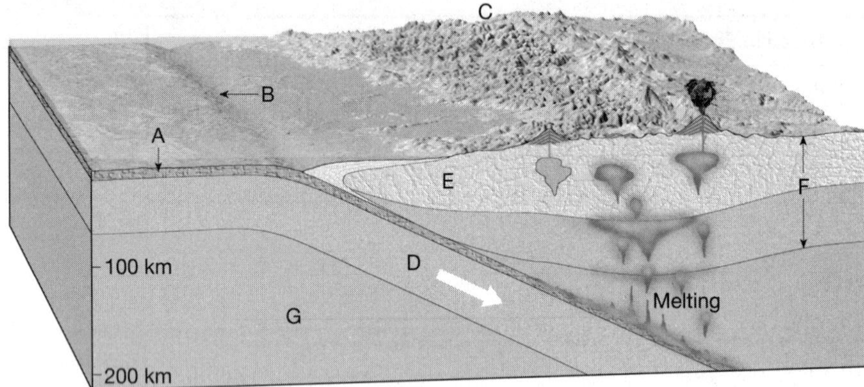

_____ Subducting oceanic lithosphere
_____ Oceanic crust
_____ Trench
_____ Continental volcanic arc
_____ Continental lithosphere
_____ Continental crust
_____ Asthenosphere

7. Newly formed land consisting of an arc-shaped island chain is called a(n) ________________.

8. Is the following sentence true or false? Mountains form as a result of a collision between two continental plates.

____

Transform Fault Boundaries

9. What happens at a transform fault boundary? ________________

____

____

10. Circle the letter of the example of a transform fault boundary that is NOT located in an ocean basin.

a. the San Andreas Fault
b. the Aleutian Trench
c. the Himalayan mountains
d. the Nazca plate

Name ______________________ Class ________________ Date ____________

Section 9.4 Mechanisms of Plate Motions

This section explains what causes plate motion and the role played by unequal distribution of heat within Earth.

Reading Strategy

Identifying Main Ideas As you read, write the main ideas for each topic. For more information on this Reading Strategy, see the **Reading and Study Skills** in the **Skills and Reference Handbook** at the end of your textbook.

Topic	Main Idea
Slab-pull	a.
Ridge-push	b.
Mantle convection	c.

What Causes Plate Motions?

1. Circle the letter of the basic force that drives plate tectonics.
   a. Earth's magnetic field
   b. convection in the mantle
   c. tidal influence of the moon
   d. radiation from the sun
2. What happens to the material involved during convection?
   ____
   ____
3. A ________________ is the continuous flow that occurs in a heated fluid becuse of differences of temperature and density.
4. The mechanism called ________________ causes oceanic lithosphere to slide down the sides of the oceanic ridge.

5. The mechanism that is the main downward component of mantle convection is ________________.

6. Is the following sentence true or false? The upward flow of material in mantle convection consists of mantle plumes of rising hot rock. ________________

7. The feature in the diagram where rock is coolest and most dense is the
   a. lower mantle
   b. descending oceanic plate
   c. rising plume
   d. oceanic ridge

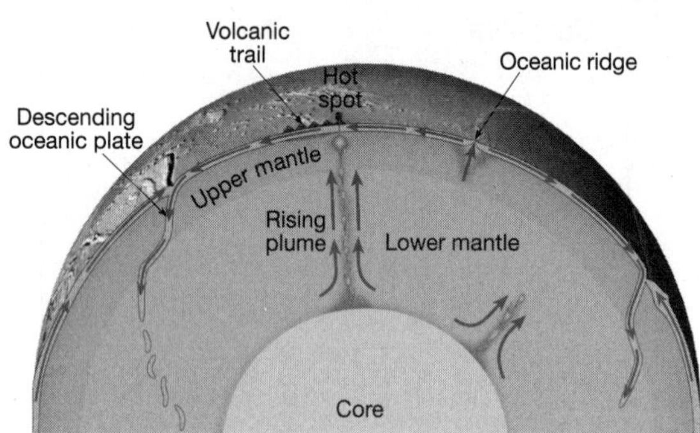

8. Circle the letter of the statement that best describes the whole-mantle convection model.
   a. Rock magnetism changes as rock layers melt under heat and pressure.
   b. Hot oceanic lithosphere descends into the mantle, and cold mantle plumes move heat toward the surface.
   c. Hot mantle plumes move heat toward the surface.
   d. Convection in Earth's molten outer core transfers heat directly to the lithosphere.

9. What causes thermal convection in the mantle?

____

____

Name ______________________ Class ________________ Date ____________

WordWise

Complete the sentences by using one of the scrambled vocabulary terms below.

gentverdi dariensbou
nagapae
chtrne
ngameopalstmie
tnegrevcon seiradnoub
nouiusbdct eozns
entlanitcno itfrd
cinocae esrigd
letasp

Destructive plate margins called ________________ are where one oceanic plate is forced down into the mantle beneath a second plate.

Where two plates move together, ________________ occur.

Wegener proposed that in the past, the continents were joined to form a supercontinent he named ________________.

________________ occur where two tectonic plates move away from each other.

An ocean ________________ is a surface feature produced by a descending plate.

Wegener's ________________ hypothesis proposed that the continents changed position on Earth's surface.

A record of ________________ is preserved in the sequence of rock strips at oceanic ridges.

Earth's lithosphere is divided into ________________ that move and change shape.

Elevated areas of the seafloor called ________________ occur along well-developed divergent plate boundaries.

Name ______________________ Class ______________ Date ____________

Section 10.1 Volcanoes and Plate Tectonics

This section explains how magma forms and discusses the relationship between plate boundaries and igneous activity.

Reading Strategy

Outlining After you read, complete the outline of the most important ideas in the section. For more information on this Reading Strategy, see the **Reading and Study Skills** in the **Skills and Reference Handbook** at the end of your textbook.

I. Origin of Magma
   - A. Heat
   - B. ______________________
   - C. ______________________

II. Volcanoes and Plate Boundaries
   - A. ______________________
   - B. ______________________
   - C. ______________________

Origin of Magma

1. Is the following sentence true or false? Magma forms when solid rock in the crust and upper mantle partially melts.

   ____

2. How is decompression melting of rocks triggered? ______________________

   ____

3. ______________ rock buried at depth has a much lower melting temperature than does ______________ rock of the same composition and under the same pressure.

Volcanoes and Plate Boundaries

4. Is the following sentence true or false? When solid mantle rock rises during seafloor spreading, magma is produced as a result of decompression melting. ______________

5. Circle the letters of the changes that allow rock melting to begin at convergent plate boundaries.
   a. decreasing pressure
   b. decreasing temperature
   c. water reducing the melting point
   d. water raising the melting point

6. What landforms develop as a result of the volcanic activity that occurs where one oceanic plate descends beneath another oceanic plate? ______________________________

7. Circle the letter of the answer that correctly completes the following sentence. At a convergent plate boundary, the fluids reduce the melting point of hot mantle rock enough for melting to begin when a sinking slab reaches a depth of about

a. 100 to 150 km. b. 500 to 550 km.
c. 700 to 750 km. d. 1000 to 1500 km.

8. Complete the concept map showing where intraplate volcanism occurs.

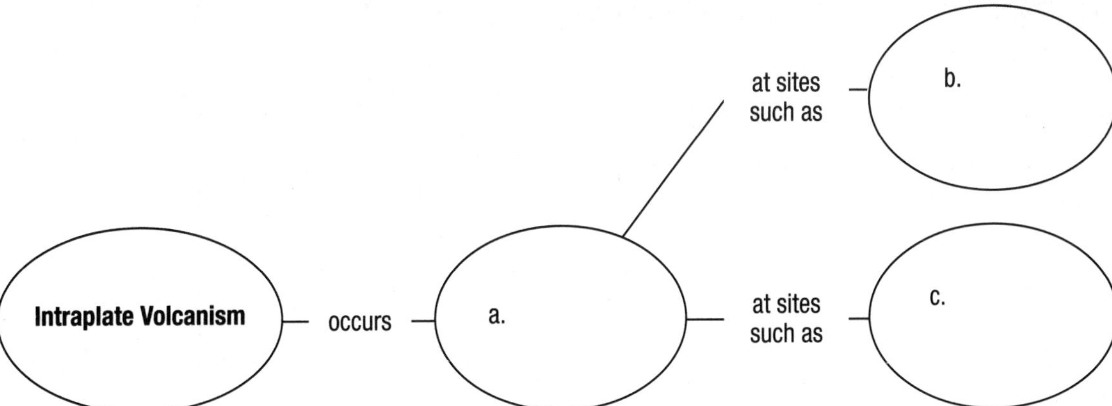

9. Circle the letter of the time most intraplate volcanism occurs.

a. when oceanic crust sinks into the mantle and melts
b. when a mantle plume rises to the surface
c. when oceanic plates separate and magma rises to fill the rift
d. when continental crust sinks into the mantle and melts

10. The result of a magma plume rising and decompression melting occurring may be the formation of a small volcanic region called a(n) ________________.

11. Circle the letter of the number of years most hot spots have lasted.

a. hundreds of years b. thousands of years
c. millions of years d. billions of years

Name ______________________ Class ____________________ Date ______________

Section 10.2 The Nature of Volcanic Eruptions

This section discusses volcanic eruptions, types of volcanoes, and other volcanic landforms.

Reading Strategy

Previewing Before you read the section, rewrite the green topic headings as questions. As you read, write the answers to the questions. For more information on this Reading Strategy, see the **Reading and Study Skills** in the **Skills and Reference Handbook** at the end of your textbook.

The Nature of Volcanic Eruptions	
What factors affect an eruption?	a.

Factors Affecting Eruptions

1. What are three factors that determine how violently or quietly a volcano erupts? ______________________________

____

____

2. Circle the letter of the term that describes lava's resistance to flow.
   a. temperature
   b. eruption
   c. viscosity
   d. basaltic

Volcanic Material

3. Is the following sentence true or false? One thing all volcanic eruptions have in common is that they emit large amounts of gas.

____

4. During a volcanic eruption, particles called ______________, ranging from very fine dust to pieces weighing several tons, are ejected.

Name ______________________ Class ______________________ Date ______________

Types of Volcanoes

5. Select the appropriate letter in the figure that identifies each of the following types of volcanoes.

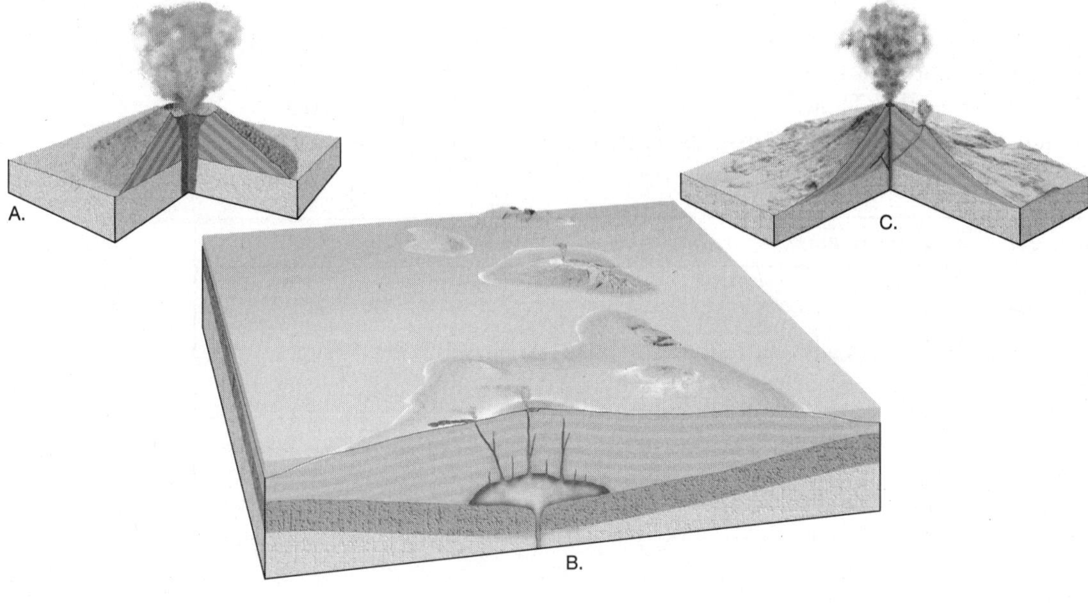

_____ shield volcano   _____ cinder cone   _____ composite cone

6. The steep-walled depression known as a(n) ________________ is located at the summit of many volcanoes.

7. Circle the letter of the type of volcano that is the product of gas-rich basaltic magma mostly in the form of loose pyroclastic material.

a. cinder cone   b. shield volcano
c. stratovolcano   d. composite cone

Other Volcanic Landforms

Match each description with its volcanic landform or feature.

Description	Volcanic Landform or Feature
_____ 8. wide area that forms when low-viscosity basaltic lava flows from fissures	a. caldera
_____ 9. rock conduit that remains when the surrounding cone has been eroded	b. lava plateau
_____ 10. depression formed by the collapse of the top of a volcano	c. volcanic neck

Volcanic Hazards

11. Is the following sentence true or false? Cinder cones are the most dangerous volcanoes. ________________

Section 10.3 Intrusive Igneous Activity

This section explains how to classify intrusive igneous features.

Reading Strategy

Comparing and Contrasting After you read, compare the types of intrusive igneous features by completing the table. For more information on this Reading Strategy, see the **Reading and Study Skills** in the **Skills and Reference Handbook** at the end of your textbook.

Types of Plutons	Description
Sill	a.
Laccolith	b.
Dike	c.
Batholith	d.

Classifying Plutons

1. Select the appropriate letter in the diagram that identifies each of the following igneous intrusive features.

   ______ sill
   ______ batholith
   ______ laccolith
   ______ dike

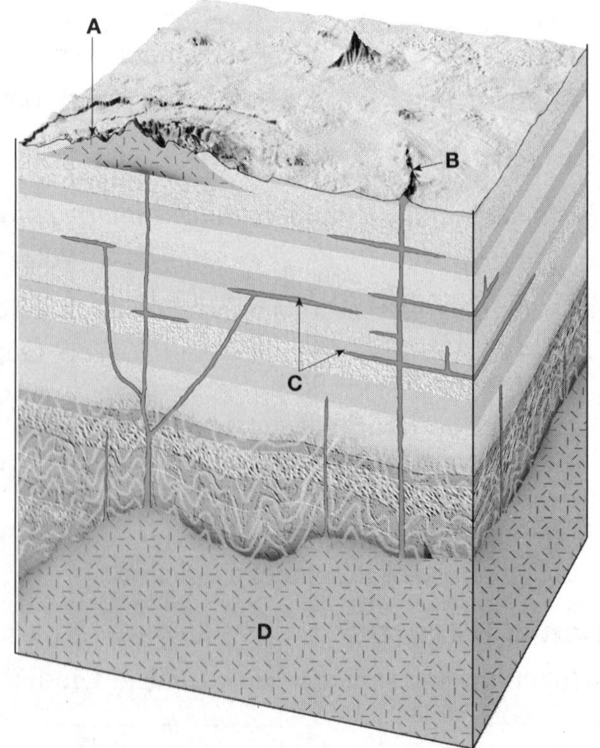

2. Is the following sentence true or false? Plutons can be studied on Earth's surface as they form.

   ____

3. What three characteristics are used to classify intrusive igneous bodies? ____

____

Match each way plutons formed with the pluton type.

	How Formed	Pluton
_____	4. when magma from a large magma chamber invades fractures in the surrounding rocks	a. sill
_____	5. when magma is injected between sedimentary layers close to Earth's surface and collects as a lens-shaped mass	b. laccolith
_____	6. when magma is injected along sedimentary bedding surfaces close to Earth's surface	c. dike

Batholiths

7. A large intrusive igneous body with an area greater than 100 km^2 exposed at the surface is called a ________________.

Name ______________________ Class ____________________ Date ____________

Section 11.1 Forces in Earth's Crust

This section explains how rocks are deformed.

Reading Strategy

Previewing Before you read, rewrite the green topic headings as how, why, and what questions. As you read, write an answer to each question. For more information on this Reading Strategy, see the **Reading and Study Skills** in the **Skills and Reference Handbook** at the end of your textbook.

Forces in Earth's Crust	
What causes deformation of rock?	
What are the types of stress?	
What is the principle of isostasy?	

Deformation of Rock

Match each definition to its term.

	Definition	Term
_____	1. the force per unit area acting on a solid	a. deformation
_____	2. the change in shape or volume of a body of rock as a result of stress	b. stress
_____	3. a general term that refers to all changes in the original shape and/or size of a body of rock	c. strain

4. What are four factors that influence the strength of a rock and how it will deform? ____

____

____

5. What are the two ways rocks permanently deform?

____

____

6. Circle the letters of the statements that are true about rock deformation.
   a. Ductile deformation is strongly aided by high temperature and high confining pressure.
   b. Small stresses applied over time play an important role in rock deformation.
   c. The mineral composition and texture of a rock affects how it will deform.
   d. Rocks near the surface usually undergo ductile deformation.

Types of Stress

7. What are the three types of stress that cause deformation of rocks?

____

____

Principle of Isostasy

8. Is the following sentence true or false? Because of accretion, deformed and thickened crust will undergo regional uplifting both during mountain building and for a long period afterward.

____

Name ______________________ Class ________________ Date __________

Chapter 11 Mountain Building

Section 11.2 Folds, Faults, and Mountains

This section explains the characteristics of various types of mountains.

Reading Strategy

Comparing and Contrasting As you read this section, compare types of faults by completing the table below.

Types of Fault	Description
Normal fault	a.
b.	c.
d.	e.
f.	g.

Folds

Match each definition to its term.

	Definition	Term
_____	**1.** large, step-like folds in otherwise horizontal sedimentary strata	a. anticlines
_____	**2.** upfolding, or arching, of rock layers	b. synclines
_____	**3.** downfolds or troughs	c. monoclines

Faults

4. Briefly describe each of the following types of faults and select the appropriate letter in the figure that identifies each fault.

Reverse fault: ______________________________

Strike-slip fault: ______________________________

Normal fault: ______________________________

Thrust fault: ______________________________

Name ____________________ Class ________________ Date ____________

Types of Mountains

Match each definition to its term.

	Definition	Term
_____	5. mountains formed primarily by folding	a. orogenesis
_____	6. the collection of processes that produce a mountain belt	b. folded mountains
_____	7. the major force that forms folded mountains	c. compressional forces

8. ________________ is also important in the formation of folded mountains, which are often called fold-and-thrust belts.

9. Circle the letter of the mountain ranges that are examples of folded mountains.
   a. Appalachian Mountains
   b. northern Rocky Mountains
   c. Teton Range in Wyoming
   d. the Alps in Europe

10. Select the letter from the figure that identifies each formation.
    _____ graben
    _____ horst

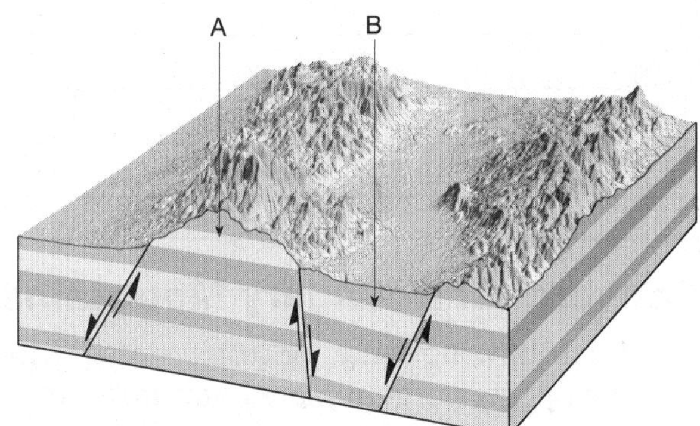

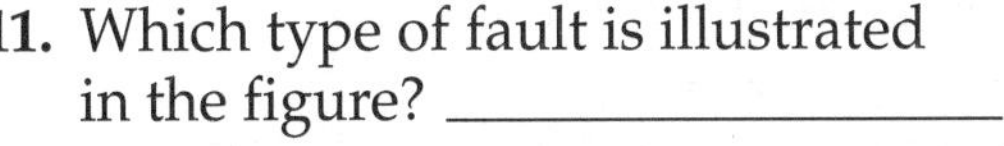

11. Which type of fault is illustrated in the figure? ________________

12. Circle the letter of each true statement about fault-block mountains.
    a. Normal faulting occurs where tensional stresses cause the crust to be stretched.
    b. Grabens produce an elongated valley bordered by horsts.
    c. The Appalachian Mountains are examples of fault-block mountains.
    d. The Basin and Range region of Nevada, Utah, and California is made of elongated grabens.

Plateaus, Domes, and Basins

13. When upwarping produces a circular or an elongated structure, the feature is called a(n) ________________.

14. Is the following sentence true or false? The Black Hills of western South Dakota make up a large domed structure thought to be formed by upwarping. ________________

15. Is the following sentence true or false? The Black Hills of South Dakota contain exposed igneous and metamorphic rock in the center of a dome. ________________

Name ______________________ Class ______________ Date __________

Section 11.3 Mountains and Plates

This section explains how mountains are formed at plate boundaries.

Reading Strategy

Outlining As you read, make an outline of the important ideas in this section. Use the green topic headings as the main topics and the blue headings as subtopics. For more information on this Reading Strategy, see the **Reading and Study Skills** in the **Skills and Reference Handbook** at the end of your textbook.

I. **Mountains and Plates**
   A. Convergent Boundary Mountains
      1. Ocean-Ocean Convergence
      2. ______________________
      3. ______________________
   B. Divergent Boundary Mountains
   C. ______________________
   D. ______________________
      1. ______________________
      2. ______________________

Convergent Boundary Mountains

1. Is the following sentence true or false? Most mountain building occurs at convergent plate boundaries. ______________

2. ______________ provide the compressional forces that fold, fault, and metamorphose the thick layers of sediment deposited at the edges of landmasses.

3. Circle the letter of each true statement about ocean-ocean convergence.

a. Ocean-ocean convergence occurs when an oceanic plate converges with a continental plate.

b. The converging plates can lead to the growth of a volcanic island arc on the ocean floor.

c. An example of an island arc formed by ocean-ocean convergence is Japan.

d. Ocean-ocean convergence mainly produces volcanic mountains.

4. Is the following sentence true or false? The types of mountains formed by ocean-continental convergence are volcanic mountains and folded mountains. ______________

5. The figure illustrates mountain building along an Andean-type subduction zone. Select the appropriate letter in the figure that identifies each of the following features.

_____ ocean trench

_____ asthenosphere

_____ continental volcanic arc

_____ accretionary wedge

_____ subducting oceanic lithosphere

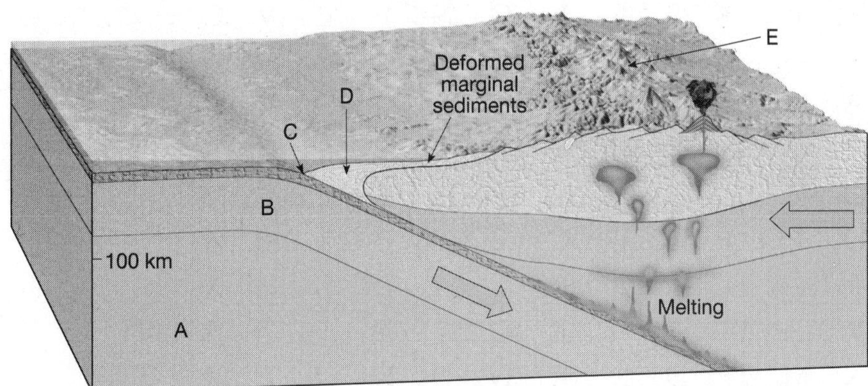

6. Is the following sentence true or false? At a convergent boundary, a collision between two plates carrying continental crust will result in the formation of folded mountains.

____

Divergent Boundary Mountains

7. __________________ mountains are formed along ocean ridges at divergent plate boundaries.

Non-Boundary Mountains

8. Why are some mountains forming at non-plate boundaries?

____

____

____

____

Continental Accretion

9. When crustal fragments called __________________ collide with a continental plate, they become stuck to or embedded into the continent in a process called __________________.

Name ______________________ Class ________________ Date ____________

Chapter 11 Mountain Building

WordWise

Solve the clues to determine which vocabulary terms from Chapter 11 are hidden in the puzzle. Then find and circle the terms in the puzzle. The terms may occur vertically, horizontally, diagonally, or backwards.

Q	A	C	C	R	E	T	I	O	N	D	S	C	A	M	A
K	L	W	O	A	U	A	V	J	E	T	N	Q	T	K	H
D	C	I	Z	Y	D	O	W	F	R	N	I	A	R	T	S
E	V	O	B	I	F	D	O	E	E	Q	N	F	P	V	G
N	I	P	L	Z	M	R	S	N	K	E	H	Y	E	N	G
I	C	D	X	B	M	S	I	S	E	N	E	G	O	R	O
L	R	K	M	A	T	L	Y	G	X	E	I	T	R	Z	B
C	J	T	T	O	C	L	J	N	N	F	H	E	Z	B	M
I	P	I	N	O	P	Q	U	E	C	Y	Y	R	X	M	W
T	O	V	N	P	Q	U	I	A	R	L	A	R	G	H	X
N	E	O	M	R	S	W	B	H	F	C	I	A	J	Z	S
A	M	P	A	X	M	U	D	S	R	W	D	N	D	L	R
Q	Z	B	S	H	F	C	M	K	P	X	J	E	E	F	K
H	E	A	J	L	Q	X	C	G	N	O	L	P	M	F	L

Clues	**Hidden Words**
The general term that refers to all changes in the shape or size of a rock body	______________
Force per unit area acting on a solid	______________
The change in shape or volume of a body of rock as a result of stress	______________
Commonly formed by the upfolding, or arching, of rock layers	______________
A trough associated with anticlines	______________
A large, step-like fold in otherwise horizontal sedimentary strata	______________
The collection of processes that produce a mountain belt	______________
Any crustal fragment that has a geologic history distinct from the adjoining accreted crustal blocks	______________
Mountains formed as large blocks of crust are uplifted and tilted along normal faults	______________
The process in which fragments become embedded or stuck to a continental plate	______________

Section 12.1 Discovering Earth's History

This section explains how geologists use rocks to interpret Earth's history.

Reading Strategy

Identifying Main Ideas As you read, fill in the first column of the table with a main idea and add details that support it in the second column. For more information on this Reading Strategy, see the **Reading and Study Skills** in the **Skills and Reference Handbook** at the end of your textbook.

Main Idea	Details
1.	
2.	
3.	
4.	
5.	

Studying Earth's History

1. What information about Earth's history do rocks record?

____

____

2. Is the following sentence true or false? By examining the rock record, we have learned that Earth is much younger than it was previously thought to be. ________________

3. The concept that the processes at work on Earth today were also at work long ago is known as the principle of ________________.

Relative Dating—Key Principles

4. Is the following sentence true or false? Scientists use relative dating to tell how long ago events occurred on Earth. ________________

5. What is the principle of original horizontality? ________________

____

____

Name ____________________ Class ____________________ Date ____________

6. Use the following figure to complete each sentence comparing the relative ages of the features. Where indicated, identify the law or principle you used to arrive at your answer.
   a. Dike B is ____________________ than fault B.
      Law or principle: ____________________
   b. The shale is ____________________ than the sandstone.
      Law or principle: ____________________
   c. Dike B is ____________________ than the batholith.
      Law or principle: ____________________
   d. The sandstone is ____________________ than Dike A.
   e. The conglomerate is ____________________ than the shale.

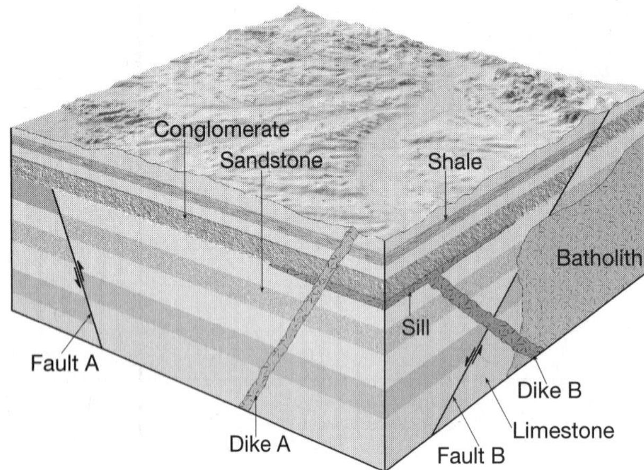

Reading the Rock Record

Match each description with its term.

	Description	Term
_____	7. represents a long period when deposition stopped, erosion occurred, and deposition resumed	a. angular unconformity
_____	8. two sedimentary rock layers separated by an erosional surface	b. disconformity
_____	9. represents a period when deformation and erosion occurred	c. unconformity

10. Circle the letter of the task of matching up rocks of similar age in different regions.
   a. correlation
   b. superposition
   c. uniformitarianism
   d. unconformity

Name ______________________ Class ________________ Date __________

Section 12.2 Fossils: Evidence of Past Life

This section discusses how fossils form and how they are used to correlate rock layers.

Reading Strategy

Monitoring Your Understanding Complete the chart. After you finish this section, correct and add details as needed. For more information on this Reading Strategy, see the **Reading and Study Skills** in the **Skills and Reference Handbook** at the end of your textbook.

Fossils	How Fossils Form	How Fossils Are Used
a.	b.	c.

1. What are fossils? ____

____

2. Is the following sentence true or false? An extinct organism is one that is still found on Earth. ________________

Types of Fossils

3. Casts are a common type of ________________.

4. Circle the letter of the type of fossil formed when an organism is buried in sediment and then dissolved by underground water.

   a. coprolite
   b. trace fossil
   c. cast
   d. mold

Match each example with its type of fossil. Some types will be used more than once.

	Example	Type of Fossil
_____	**5.** frozen mammoth	a. preserved remains
_____	**6.** animal footprint	b. trace fossil
_____	**7.** fly in amber	

Conditions for Fossilization

8. Complete the following concept map showing conditions that favor the preservation of fossils.

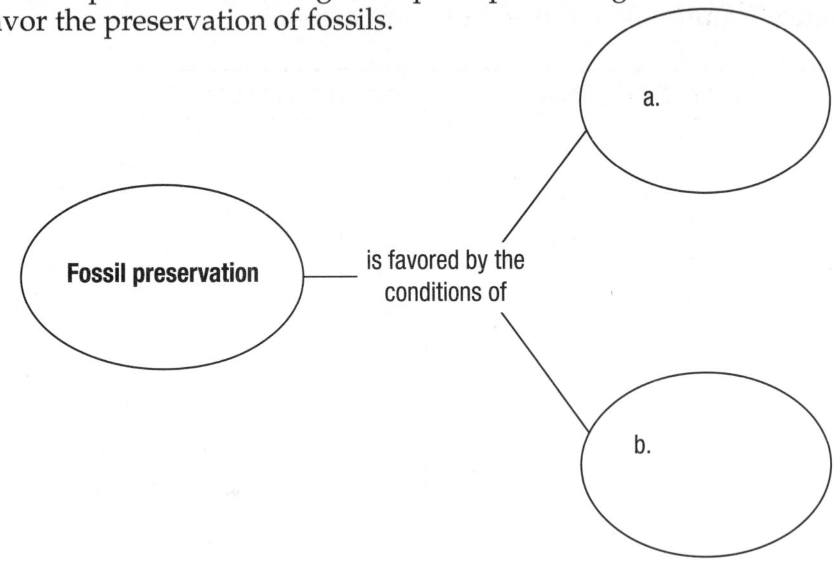

Fossils and the History of Life

9. Fossil organisms succeed each other in an order that is definite and determinable according to the principle of ________________.

10. According to Darwin's theory of evolution, one species can evolve into another through the process of ________________.

Interpreting the Fossil Record

11. What are index fossils? ____

____

____

____

____

____

12. Is the following sentence true or false? Scientists use fossils to interpret and describe ancient environments. ________________

Section 12.3 Dating With Radioactivity

This section explains how radioactivity is used to determine the age of rocks.

Reading Strategy

Monitoring Your Understanding Preview the key concepts, topics, headings, vocabulary, and figures in this section. List two things you expect to learn about each. After reading, state what you learned about each item you listed. For more information on this Reading Strategy, see the **Reading and Study Skills** in the **Skills and Reference Handbook** at the end of your textbook.

What I expect to learn	What I learned
1.	
2.	

What Is Radioactivity?

1. Is the following sentence true or false? Isotopes of the same element have different numbers of neutrons. ________________

2. The process by which unstable nuclei spontaneously decay is known as ________________.

3. Circle the letter of the final result of radioactive decay.

a. parent element
b. radioactive isotope
c. stable daughter product
d. unstable daughter product

4. Circle the letter of what decays first during radioactive decay.

a. parent element
b. stable isotope
c. stable daughter product
d. unstable daughter product

Name ______________________ Class ______________ Date __________

Use the graph to answer the following three questions.

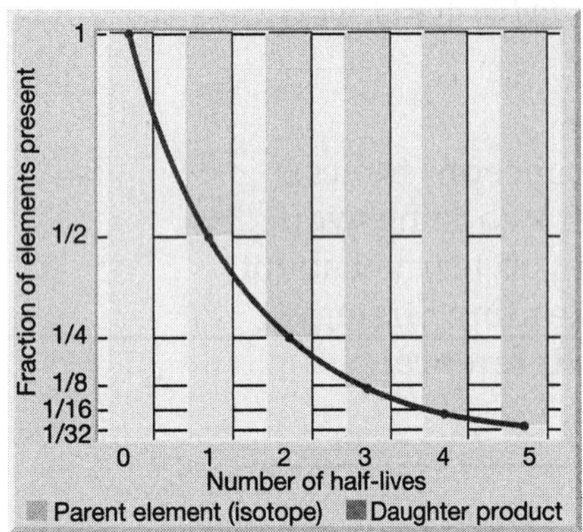

5. After one half-life, what fraction of the parent element has decayed to a daughter product? ______________

6. After three half-lives, what fraction of the daughter product has formed?
____

7. How many half-lives must pass before only 1/32 of the parent element remains undecayed to a daughter product? ______________

Radiometric Dating

8. The procedure called ______________ provides a way to determine the ages of rocks that contain certain radioactive isotopes.

9. Is the following sentence true or false? A radioactive isotope decays at a varying rate from the time it forms. ______________

10. What begins to happen to radioactive uranium as soon as a mineral containing it crystallizes from magma? ______________
____

11. What conditions are needed for an accurate radiometric date to be obtained from a mineral sample? ______________
____
____

Dating with Carbon-14

12. Circle the letter of the ratio of two substances that is compared in a sample of a dead organism during radiocarbon dating.
    a. carbon-12 to uranium 238
    b. carbon-14 to carbon-12
    c. uranium-238 to lead-206
    d. uranium-238 to carbon-12

13. Is the following sentence true or false? Radiometric dating is rarely used to determine the age of sedimentary rocks.
____

Name ______________________ Class ________________ Date __________

Section 12.4 The Geologic Time Scale

This section discusses the geologic time scale and difficulties with constructing it.

Reading Strategy

Outlining As you read, complete the outline of the important ideas in this section. Use the green headings as the main topics and fill in details from the remainder of the text. For more information on this Reading Strategy, see the **Reading and Study Skills** in the **Skills and Reference Handbook** at the end of your textbook.

I. Structure of the Time Scale
   A. ______________________
      a. geologic time scale: ______________________
      ____
      b. eon: ______________________
      c. Precambrian time: ______________________
   B. ______________________
      d. era: ______________________
   C. ______________________
      e. period: ______________________
      f. epoch: ______________________

1. What is the geologic time scale? ______________________

____

____

Structure of the Time Scale

2. Complete the following flowchart with the types of subdivisions of the geologic time scale, from longest to shortest expanse of time.

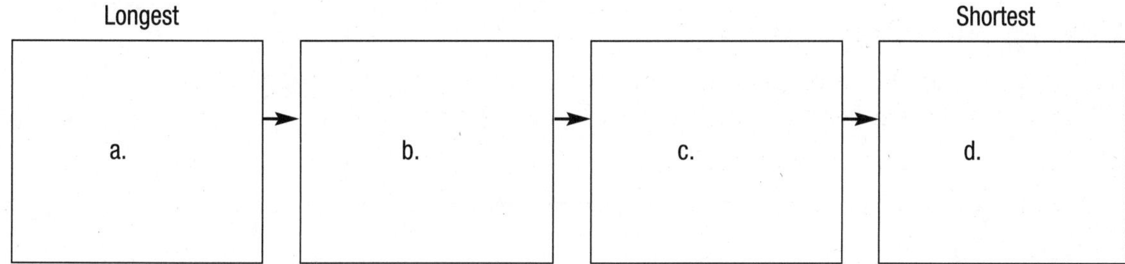

3. Is the following sentence true or false? The Precambrian represents a much longer part of Earth's history than the Phanerozoic.
____

4. Why do geologists know so little about Precambrian history?
____
____
____

5. The Precambrian time starts at ______________ and continues until the start of the ______________ period over 4 billion years later.

6. Circle the approximate percentage of the geologic time scale that Precambrian time comprises.

   a. 44 percent
   b. 50 percent
   c. 73 percent
   d. 88 percent

7. The eon called the ______________ began about 540 million years ago.

8. Circle the letter of the eras into which the Phanerozoic is divided.

   a. epoch, period, eon
   b. Proterozoic, Archean, Hadean
   c. Triassic, Jurassic, Cretaceous
   d. Paleozoic, Mesozoic, Cenozoic

9. Is the following sentence true or false? Periods such as the Tertiary are characterized by more profound life-form changes than those of eras. ______________

Name ______________________ Class ________________ Date ___________

WordWise

Test your knowledge of vocabulary terms from Chapter 12 by completing this crossword puzzle.

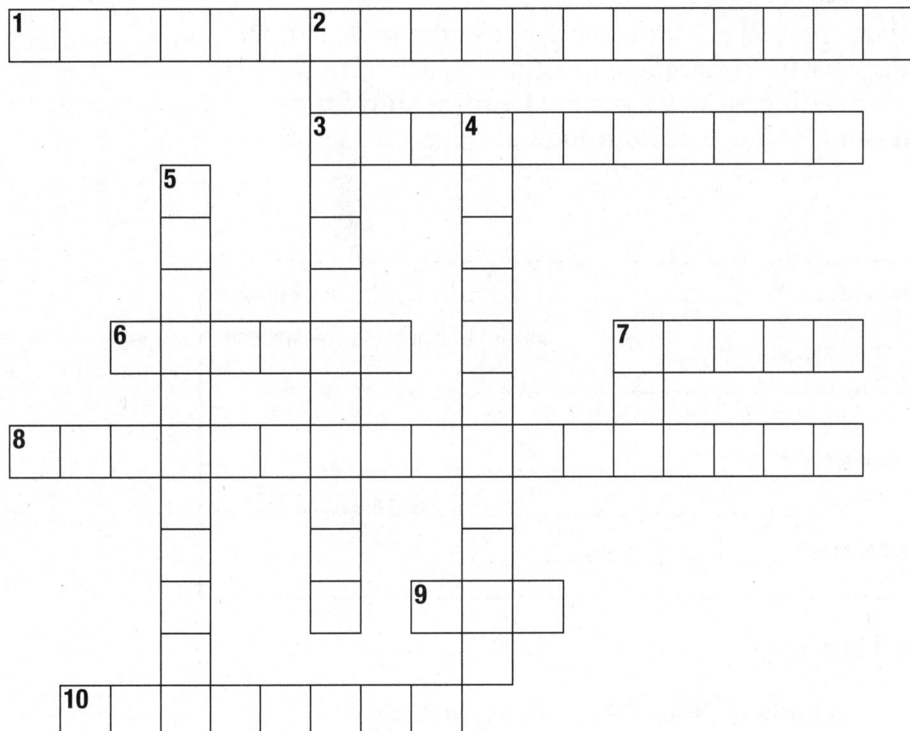

Clues across:

1. states that in an undeformed sequence of sedimentary rocks, each bed is older than the one above it
3. task of matching up rocks of similar age in different regions
6. subdivision of an era
7. shorter than a period on the geologic time scale
8. principle that states that the same physical, chemical, and biological laws operate today as in the past
9. greatest expanse of time on the geologic time scale
10. time when one half of a parent isotope is decayed

Clues down:

7. expanse of time (example: Paleozoic)
2. represents a break in the rock record
4. ________ dating: method of using carbon-14 to find the age of dead organisms
5. time indicator that is a particularly useful means of correlating rocks of similar age in different regions

Name ______________________ Class ________________ Date __________

Section 13.1 Precambrian Time

This section discusses Earth's history during the Precambrian time.

Reading Strategy

Building Vocabulary As you read this section, use the information about the vocabulary terms to complete these phrases. For more information on this Reading Strategy, see the **Reading and Study Skills** in the **Skills and Reference Handbook** at the end of your textbook.

1. Shields are composed of a. ______________________; are evidence of b. ______________________; and are significant to Precambrian time because c. ______________________.

2. Stromatolites are composed of d. ______________________; are evidence of e. ______________________; and are significant to Precambrian time because f. ______________________.

Precambrian Earth

1. Explain why little is known about Precambrian history.

____

____

____

____

____

____

____

Match each description to its term.

	Description	**Term**
_____	**2.** organisms that changed the atmosphere	a. shields
_____	**3.** large core areas of Precambrian rocks that make up the surface of some continents	b. cyanobacteria
_____	**4.** source of information about Precambrian rocks	c. ores
_____	**5.** some of Earth's oldest rocks	d. greenstone

6. Complete the following flowchart.

How Earth's Atmosphere Changed Over Time

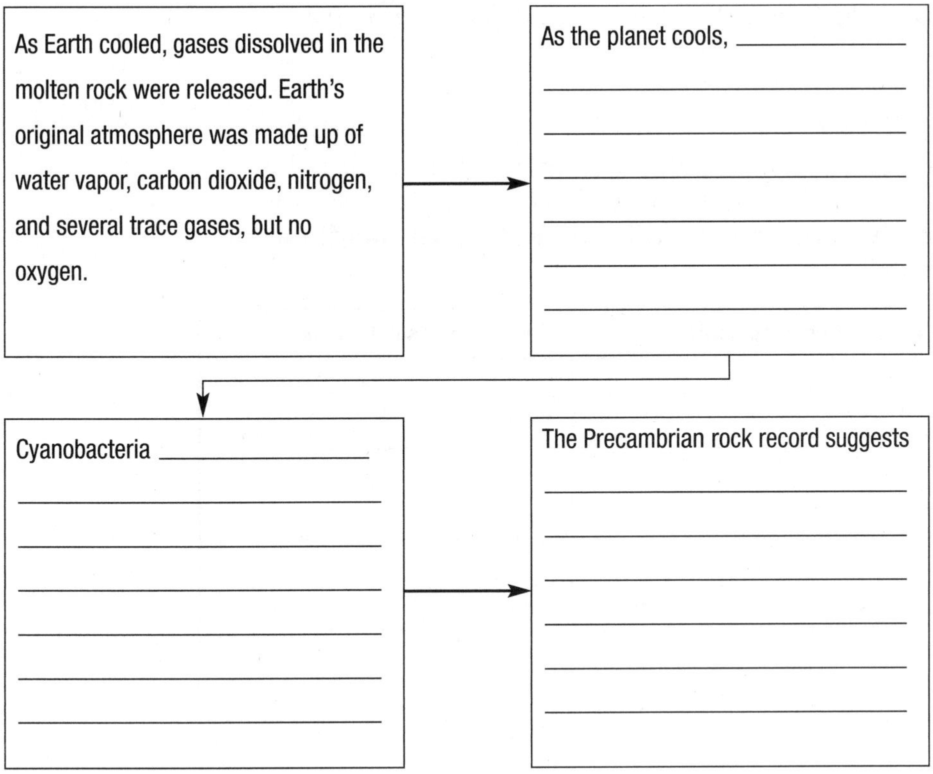

As Earth cooled, gases dissolved in the molten rock were released. Earth's original atmosphere was made up of water vapor, carbon dioxide, nitrogen, and several trace gases, but no oxygen. →	As the planet cools, ______________________
↓	
Cyanobacteria ______________________ →	The Precambrian rock record suggests ______________________

Precambrian Life

7. Circle the letter of each sentence that is true about Precambrian fossils.
   a. Precambrian fossils made by cyanobacteria are stromatolites.
   b. Prokaryotes evolved before eukaryotes.
   c. Cyanobacteria are eukaryotes.
   d. Animal fossils date to the early Precambrian time.

8. Is the following sentence true or false? Stromatolites are trace fossils. ______________

Section 13.2 Paleozoic Era: Life Explodes

This section explains the changes that took place on Earth during the Paleozoic era.

Reading Strategy

Identifying Details As you read this section, fill in the table below with notes. For more information on this Reading Strategy, see the **Reading and Study Skills** in the **Skills and Reference Handbook** at the end of your textbook.

Period	Geologic Developments	Developments in Life Forms
Cambrian		
Ordovician		
Silurian		

1. What is a mass extinction?

____

2. What is the first period of the Paleozoic?

____

Ordovician Period

3. During the Ordovician, the first ________________ plants evolved.

Silurian Period

4. Circle the letter of each sentence that is true about the Silurian.
   a. During the Silurian, Gondwana encompassed parts of five continents: South America, Africa, Australia, Antarctica, and parts of Asia.
   b. During the Silurian period, much of North America was covered by shallow seas.
   c. During the Silurian period, large barrier reefs restricted circulation between shallow marine basins and the open ocean.

5. Using the figure, write the name of the present-day region as it appeared on the continent of Gondwana during the early Paleozoic next to each letter.

   A ________________ B ________________

   C ________________ D ________________

   E ________________ F ________________

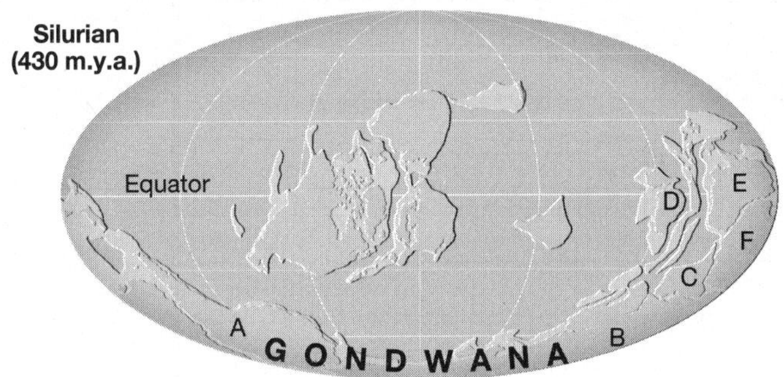

Devonian Period

6. Is the following sentence true or false? The continent of Laurasia was composed of the present-day continents of North America, Europe, and Australia. ________________

Carboniferous Period

7. Among the animals that evolved during the Carboniferous were the first ________________.

Permian Period

8. Is the following sentence true or false? As the Permian period began, all the continents had fused into the supercontinent of Pangaea. ________________

9. What are two hypotheses about the mass extinction of species that ended the Permian?

____

____

____

____

Section 13.3 Mesozoic Era: Age of Reptiles

This section describes the changes that took place during the Mesozoic era.

Reading Strategy

Summarizing As you read, write a brief summary of the text for each heading. For more information on this Reading Strategy, see the **Reading and Study Skills** in the **Skills and Reference Handbook** at the end of your textbook.

I. Triassic Period
- Supercontinent Pangaea forms.
- First dinosaurs evolve.

____

____

____

____

____

____

____

____

____

____

1. What were the three periods that divided the Mesozoic era?

____

Triassic Period

2. Circle the letter of each sentence that is true about the Triassic period.
   a. When the Triassic began, much of the world's land was in one supercontinent.
   b. Very few plant fossils were found from the Triassic period.
   c. A major event of the Triassic was the formation of Pangaea.
   d. Toward the end of the Triassic, mammals evolved.
3. Is the following sentence true or false? Gymnosperms became common during the Triassic. _______________

4. Complete the following table.

Changes During the Triassic Period	
Continental positions	
Plant life	
Animal life	

Jurassic Period

5. What were some unusual features of the ichthyosaurs and the plesiosaurs? ____

____

Cretaceous Period

6. Is the following sentence true or false? All dinosaurs were large.

____

7. Is the following sentence true or false? Angiosperms evolved during the Cretaceous. ______________

The Cretaceous Extinction

8. Explain the chain of events that may have occurred if a meteorite collided with Earth, causing the extinction of many plants and animals.

____

____

____

____

Name ______________________ Class ______________ Date __________

Section 13.4 Cenozoic Era: Age of Mammals

This section describes the changes that took place during the Cenozoic era.

Reading Strategy

Monitoring Your Understanding Preview the Key Concepts, topic headings, vocabulary, and figures in this section. List two things you expect to learn about each. After reading, state what you learned about each item listed. For more information on this Reading Strategy, see the **Reading and Study Skills** in the **Skills and Reference Handbook** at the end of your textbook.

What I Expect to Learn	What I Learned

The Age of Mammals

1. Circle the letter of the dominant land animals during the Cenozoic era.
   a. reptiles b. mammals c. amphibians d. insects
2. Is the following sentence true or false? The Cenozoic period is often called the "age of mammals." ______________.
3. Complete the following chart.

Contrasting Mammals and Reptiles	
Mammals	**Reptiles**
a. have body hair	
b.	are cold-blooded
c. have adaptations to survive in cold regions	

4. Is the following sentence true or false? The adaptations of mammals allow them to lead more active lives than reptiles. ______________

Tertiary Period

5. Is the following sentence true or false? Plate interactions during the Tertiary caused many events including mountain building.
____

6. Is the following sentence true or false? Grasses developed and spread rapidly over the plains during the Tertiary.
_______________.

7. What are three adaptations of teeth in mammals?
   a. _______________
   b. _______________
   c. _______________

Quaternary Period

8. Circle the letter of each sentence that is true about mammals during the Quaternary.
   a. Milankovitch cycles provide a partial explanation for recent ice ages.
   b. Many very large mammals evolved.
   c. Saber-toothed cats that evolved during this era can be found in some parts of Asia today.
   d. The mastodon and mammoth died because of major glacial advances.

9. What may have caused the extinctions of large mammals at the end of the last ice age?
____
____

Name ______________________ Class ________________ Date ____________

Chapter 14 The Ocean Floor

Section 14.1 The Vast World Ocean

This section discusses how much of Earth is covered by water and how that water is studied.

Reading Strategy

Building Vocabulary As you read the section, define each term in the table in your own words. For more information on this Reading Strategy, see the **Reading and Study Skills** in the **Skills and Reference Handbook** at the end of your textbook.

Vocabulary Term	Definition
oceanography	a.
bathymetry	b.
sonar	c.
submersible	d.

The Blue Planet

1. Is the following sentence true or false? The science of oceanography includes the study of the geological, chemical, physical, and biological characteristics of the world ocean. ______________

2. Circle the letter of the percentage of Earth's surface covered by the global ocean.

   a. 11 percent b. 29 percent
   c. 71 percent d. 99 percent

Geography of the Oceans

Match each description with its ocean.

	Description	Ocean
_____	**3.** shallowest ocean	a. Pacific
_____	**4.** located almost entirely in the Southern Hemisphere	b. Atlantic
_____	**5.** about half the size of the Pacific	c. Indian
_____	**6.** largest and deepest ocean	d. Arctic

7. Using the following map, list the names of Earth's four main ocean basins from smallest to largest.

   a. ______________
   b. ______________
   c. ______________
   d. ______________

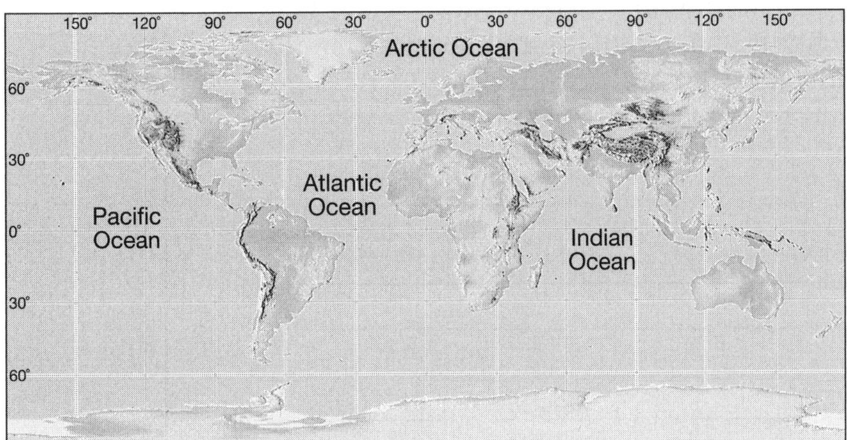

8. Looking at the map, what ocean(s) does 0° longitude intersect?

   ____

9. Look at the map and then circle the letter of the location of the Indian Ocean.

   a. 1°N 1°W
   b. 30°N 30°W
   c. 30°S 150°W
   d. 30°S 90°E

Mapping the Ocean Floor

10. Is the following sentence true or false? The ocean floor's topography is much less diverse than that of the continents.

    ____

11. What do scientists call the charting of the ocean floor and the measurement of its depths? ______________

12. Electronic depth-sounding equipment called ______________ allowed scientists in the 1920s and later to precisely measure ocean depth.

13. How are satellites used to measure ocean surface height?

    ____

    ____

14. Is the following sentence true or false? Submersibles make it possible for scientists to collect data from areas of the ocean that were previously unreachable. ______________

Name ______________________ Class ________________ Date ____________

Section 14.2 Ocean Floor Features

This section discusses the features found in the three main regions of Earth's ocean floor.

Reading Strategy

Outlining In the outline, use the green headings as the main topics and the blue headings as subtopics. As you read, add supporting details. For more information on this Reading Strategy, see the **Reading and Study Skills** in the **Skills and Reference Handbook** at the end of your textbook.

I. Continental Margins
   A. Continental Shelf
   B. Continental Slope
   C. ______________________
II. ______________________
   A. ______________________
   ____
   ____
____
   ____
   ____

1. What are the three ocean floor regions that have their own unique characteristics? ______________________

____

Continental Margins

2. A(n) ________________ can best be described as a transition zone between an ocean basin floor and a continent.

3. What covers the Atlantic Ocean's continental margin?

____

____

4. Is the following sentence true or false? The continental margin of the Pacific Ocean has very little volcanic or earthquake activity.

____

Name ______________________ Class ________________ Date __________

5. Write the letter of each of the following features of the continental margin shown in the figure.

_____ submarine canyon

_____ continental slope

_____ continental shelf

_____ continental rise

6. What economic and political significance do continental shelves have? ______________________________

____

____

7. Circle the letter of occasional movements down the continental slope of dense water rich in sediment.

a. submarine flows

b. turbidity currents

c. continental rises

d. guyots

Ocean Basin Floor

8. Is the following sentence true or false? The area covered by the ocean basin floor is comparable to the percentage of land on Earth's surface that is above sea level. ________________

Match each description with its ocean feature.

	Description	Ocean Feature
_____	9. submerged volcanic peak	a. abyssal plain
_____	10. submerged, flat-topped peak	b. guyot
_____	11. crease in the ocean floor formed where one plate plunges beneath another	c. seamount
_____	12. flat feature formed when suspended sediments settle from turbidity currents	d. trench

Mid-Ocean Ridges

13. Circle the letter of the location where new ocean floor forms.

a. mid-ocean ridge b. trench

c. continental shelf d. continental rise

14. ________________ is the moving apart of two plates at divergent plate boundaries.

Section 14.3 Seafloor Sediments

This section describes three types of ocean floor sediments.

Reading Strategy

Summarizing Complete the table with all the headings for the section. Write a brief summary of the text for each heading. For more information on this Reading Strategy, see the **Reading and Study Skills** in the **Skills and Reference Handbook** at the end of your textbook.

Actions at Boundaries
I. Types of Seafloor Sediments • Terrigenous sediments originated on land. ______________ ______________ ______________ ______________ ______________ • Biogenous sediments are biological in origin. ______________ ______________ ______________ ______________ ______________ • ______________ ______________ ______________ ______________ ______________

1. Is the following sentence true or false? In general, as you move from the continental shelf toward the deep-ocean floor, sediments become coarser. ______________

2. Circle the letter of the usual amount of seafloor sediments in a given location.

   a. about 100 to 450 m b. about 500 to 1000 m
   c. about 100 to 450 km d. about 500 to 1000 km

Types of Seafloor Sediments

3. Circle the letters of the three categories of ocean floor sediments.

   a. terrigenous sediment b. biogenous sediment
   c. manganese sediment d. hydrogenous sediment

Name ______________________ Class ________________ Date ____________

Match how each sediment forms with its type of sediment.

	How Sediment Forms	**Type of Sediment**
_____	**4.** crystallizes directly from ocean water through chemical reactions	a. hydrogenous
_____	**5.** accumulates on the ocean floor after erosion and transportation from land	b. terrigenous
_____	**6.** accumulates on the ocean floor when marine animals and algae die and their hard parts sink	c. biogenous

7. Complete the following chart with the types and descriptions of how the three types of hydrogenous sediments form.

Types of Hydrogenous Sediments	How They Form

8. Biogenous sediment called ____________________ consists mostly of shells of radiolarians and diatoms.

9. Circle the letter of a material that, when buried and hardened, becomes a type of limestone.

a. evaporites
b. radiolarians
c. calcareous ooze
d. calcium carbonates

10. Ocean sediment made up of the calcium carbonate shells of marine organisms is called ____________________.

11. Is the following sentence true or false? Ocean-floor sediments are usually mixtures of the various sediment types.

____

Section 14.4 Resources From the Seafloor

This section discusses the energy and mineral resources obtained from Earth's seafloor.

Reading Strategy

Identifying Details As you read, complete the concept map to identify details about resources from the ocean. For more information on this Reading Strategy, see the **Reading and Study Skills** in the **Skills and Reference Handbook** at the end of your textbook.

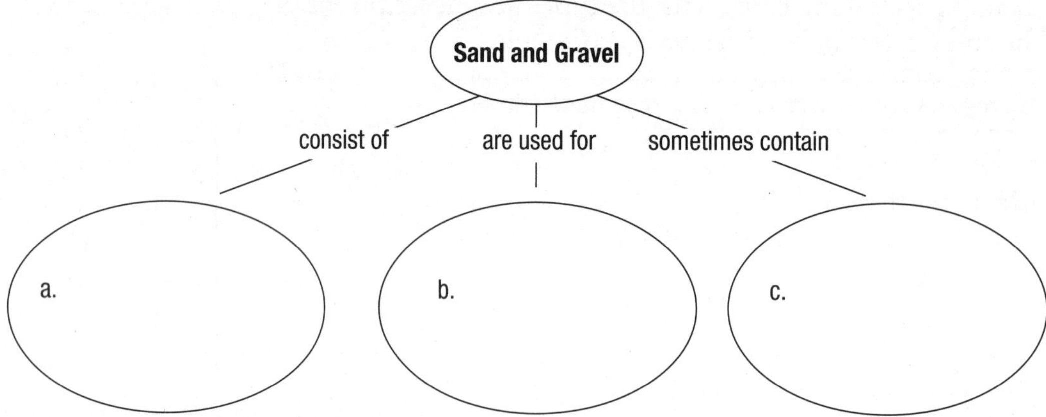

Energy Resources

1. Circle the letter of the main energy products currently being obtained from the seafloor.
   a. gas hydrates and salts
   b. coal and oil
   c. natural gas and gas hydrates
   d. natural gas and oil

2. The source of today's natural gas and oil deposits is the ancient remains of microscopic ________________.

3. Is the following sentence true or false? The majority of the world's oil is produced from ocean floor resources. ________________

4. What is one environmental concern about offshore petroleum exploration? ____

____

____

5. Compact chemical structures made of water and natural gas under the ocean floor are called ________________.

6. How do gas hydrates form? ______________________________________

7. Is the following sentence true or false? When brought up from the ocean floor to the ocean surface, gas hydrates rapidly break down. ________________

Other Resources

8. Circle the letter of the method of obtaining sand and gravel from the ocean.
   a. drilling offshore
   b. mining with suction devices
   c. collecting with submersibles
   d. evaporating from ocean water

9. How do manganese nodules form? ______________________________________

10. Complete the following flowchart to show how evaporative salts form.

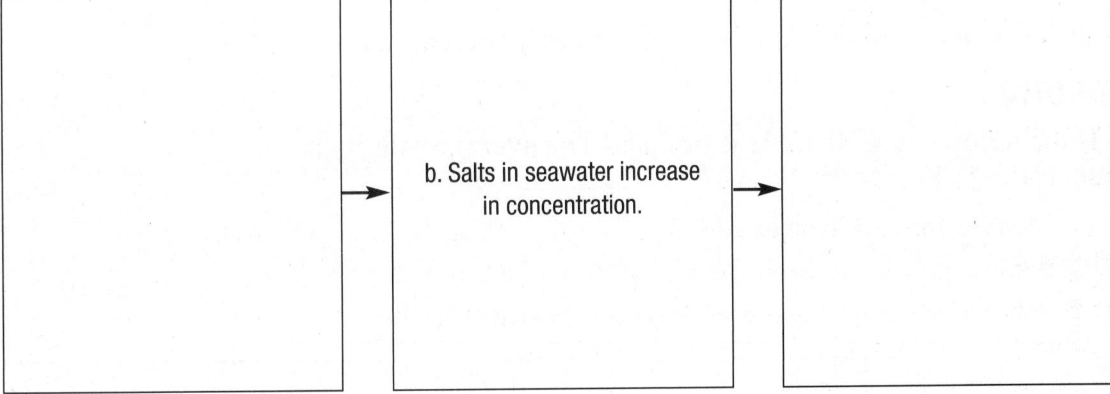

Name ______________________ Class ______________________ Date ______________

Section 15.1 The Composition of Seawater

This section describes substances found in seawater, the temperature profiles of oceans, and the density profiles of oceans.

Reading Strategy

Previewing Before you read, preview the figures in this section and add three more questions to the table. As you read, write the answers to your questions. For more information on this Reading Strategy, see the **Reading and Study Skills** in the **Skills and Reference Handbook** at the end of your textbook.

Questions About Seawater	Answers
What processes affect seawater salinity?	a.
b.	c.
d.	e.
f.	g.

1. Circle the letter of each sentence that is true about seawater.
   a. Seawater contains dissolved substances that give it a salty taste.
   b. Sodium chloride, other salts, metals, and gases are dissolved in seawater.
   c. Every known naturally occurring element is found in at least trace amounts in seawater.
   d. Seawater is suitable for drinking and irrigation of crops.

Salinity

2. Is the following sentence true or false? The average salinity of seawater is 35 percent. ______________

3. Most of the salt in seawater is ______________, or common table salt.

4. What are two sources of dissolved substances in the ocean? ____

____

5. How do elements from Earth's interior get into seawater?

____

____

Ocean Water and Ocean Life

6. What are four ways in which fresh water is naturally added to seawater, decreasing its salinity? ______________

____

7. What are two natural processes that increase the salinity of seawater? ______________

Ocean Temperature Variation

8. Is the following sentence true or false? The ocean's surface water temperature varies with the amount of solar radiation received, which is primarily a function of longitude. ______________

9. Using the following graph, what temperature is seawater below 1500 m in the low latitudes? ______________

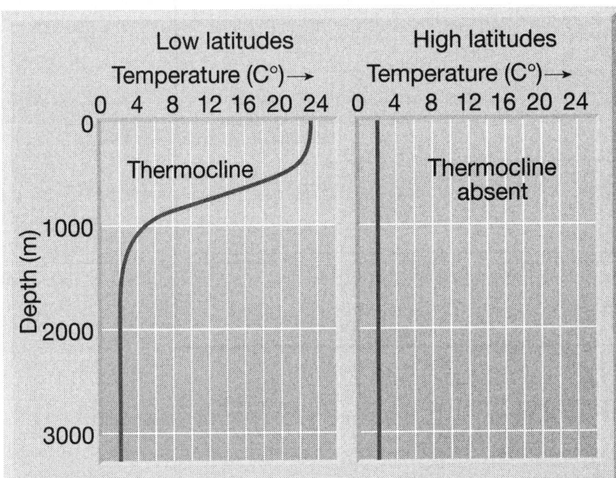

10. What is the temperature profile of seawater in the high latitudes, according to the graph? ______________

Ocean Density Variation

11. Circle the letters of the two main factors that influence density of seawater.
    a. salinity
    b. temperature
    c. pycnocline
    d. thermocline

12. Circle the letter of the ocean layer where there is a rapid change of density with depth.
    a. surface zone
    b. thermocline
    c. pycnocline
    d. transition zone

Ocean Layering

13. Is the following sentence true or false? Oceanographers generally recognize a three-layered structure in most parts of the open ocean: a shallow surface mixed zone, a transition zone, and a deep zone. ______________

Name ______________________ Class ______________ Date __________

Chapter 15 **Ocean Water and Ocean Life**

Section 15.2 The Diversity of Ocean Life

This section describes the diversity of organisms found in the ocean.

Reading Strategy

Building Vocabulary As you read, add definitions and examples to complete the table below. For more information on this Reading Strategy, see the **Reading and Study Skills** in the **Skills and Reference Handbook** at the end of your textbook.

Definitions	Examples
Plankton: organisms that drift with ocean currents	bacteria
Phytoplankton: a.	b.
Zooplankton: c.	d.
Nekton: e.	f.
Benthos: g.	h.

1. What organism directly or indirectly provides food for the majority of organisms? ______________

Classification of Marine Organisms

2. How are marine organisms classified? ______________________________

____

____

Match each classification to its example.

	Classification	**Example**
_____	**3.** plankton	a. adult sea star
_____	**4.** nekton	b. diatom
_____	**5.** benthos	c. salmon

Marine Life Zones

6. What are the three factors used to divide the ocean into distinct marine life zones? ______________________________

____

____

7. Circle the letter of each sentence that is true about life in the ocean.
   a. In the euphotic zone, phytoplankton use sunlight to produce food.
   b. Phytoplankton is the basis of most oceanic food webs.
   c. Photosynthesis occurs from the surface to deep into the abyssal zone of the ocean.
   d. The neritic zone covers about 5 percent of the world's ocean, but supports 90 percent of the world's commercial fisheries.

8. Using the figure, select the letter that identifies each of the following marine life zones.

   _____ euphotic zone

   _____ neritic zone

   _____ aphotic zone

   _____ abyssal zone

   _____ photic zone

   _____ pelagic zone

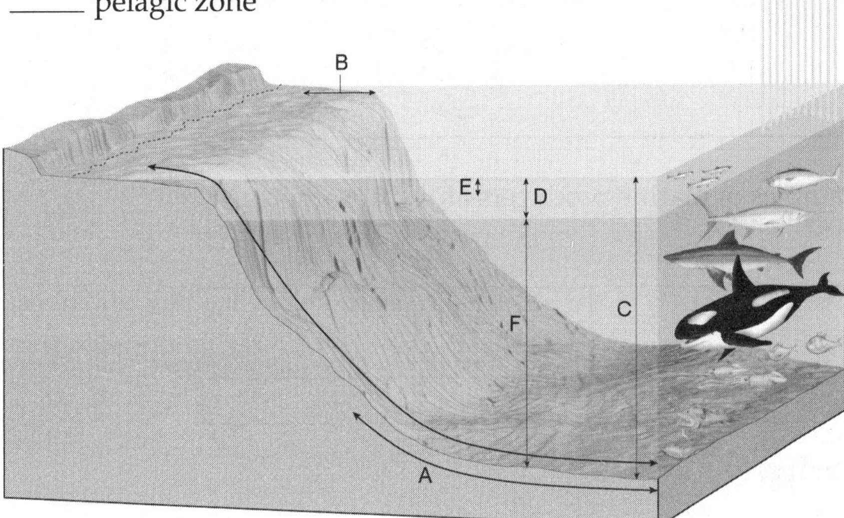

Hydrothermal Vents

9. What is a hydrothermal vent? _______________________________________

____

____

10. What is unusual about life and these hydrothermal vents?

____

____

____

Section 15.3 Oceanic Productivity

This section explains the productivity of different regions of the ocean.

Reading Strategy

Identifying Main Ideas As you read this section, write the main idea of each topic below. For more information on this Reading Strategy, see the **Reading and Study Skills** in the **Skills and Reference Handbook** at the end of your textbook.

Topic	Main Idea
Productivity in polar oceans	a.
Productivity in tropical oceans	b.
Productivity in temperate oceans	c.

1. What are two examples of marine producers and six examples of marine consumers?

Producers: ____

____

Consumers: ____

____

Primary Productivity

Match each description to its term.

Description

_____ **2.** the use of light energy to convert water and carbon dioxide into energy-rich glucose molecules

_____ **3.** the production of organic compounds from inorganic substances through photosynthesis or chemosynthesis

_____ **4.** the process by which certain microorganisms create organic molecules from inorganic nutrients, using chemical energy

Term

a. primary productivity

b. photosynthesis

c. chemosynthesis

5. What two factors influence a region's photosynthetic productivity? ______________________

____

6. What limits photosynthetic productivity in polar areas?

____

____

7. Is the following sentence true or false? Productivity in tropical regions is unlimited because of the abundance of nutrients.

____

8. What limits productivity in tropical oceans? ______________________

____

____

Oceanic Feeding Relationships

9. Approximately what percentage of light energy absorbed by algae is changed into food and made available to herbivores?

____

10. Using the figure, select the letter that identifies each of the following transfer efficiencies in the ecosystem shown.

_____ 1 unit becomes tropic level 5 (human) biomass

_____ 10,000 units of radiant energy are converted to tropic level 1 (phytoplankton) biomass

_____ 100 units become tropic level 3 biomass

_____ 1000 units become tropic level 2 (zooplankton) biomass

_____ 10 units become tropic level 4 biomass

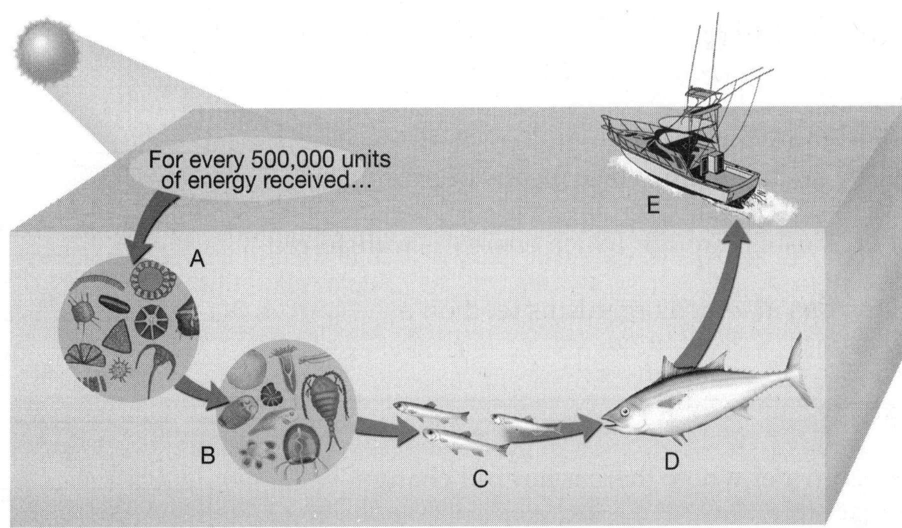

11. What percentage of energy is transferred from the sun to level 5?

____

Name ______________________ Class __________________ Date ____________

Chapter 15 Ocean Water and Ocean Life

WordWise

Solve the clues to determine which vocabulary terms from Chapter 15 are hidden in the puzzle. Then find and circle the terms in the puzzle. The terms may occur vertically, horizontally, diagonally, or backward.

F P Z Y A R U M Q G E F D F G
O I Y T Z O V F Z N P S P V D
O E M C T R O P I C L E V E L
D T B R N K U L S S M V K L B
C E D Z G O C E A T U F I J Z
H X X B W O C L Q X Q Q C L O
A B K J M H I L I G J T Y W M
I Q E R P N C N I V X S I S S
N H E W I Y I T W N O Q R Q V
O H L T D S G S Q U E K J S X
T J Y A O O X U O N M D Y O E
K T A V E R O N O T K N A L P
E S L R P F L F Z S U F U M H
N S M Y M O X W G W J S H M U
B T P B J M N A S I P B Z R O

Clues	**Hidden Words**
The total amount of solid material dissolved in water	________________
The layer of ocean where there is a rapid change of temperature with depth	________________
Organisms that drift with ocean currents	________________
Animals capable of moving independently of the ocean currents, by swimming or other means of propulsion	________________
A sequence of organisms through which energy is transferred	________________
Feeding relationships in which organisms feed on a variety of organisms	________________
A feeding stage	________________
The layer of ocean water where there is a rapid change of density with depth	________________

Section 16.1 Ocean Circulation

This section discusses how movements of surface and deep-ocean waters occur.

Reading Strategy

Identifying Main Ideas As you read, write the main idea of each topic in the table. For more information on this Reading Strategy, see the **Reading and Study Skills** in the **Skills and Reference Handbook** at the end of your textbook.

Topic	Main Idea
Surface currents	a.
Gyres	b.
Ocean currents and climate	c.
Upwelling	d.

Surface Circulation

1. Is the following sentence true or false? Friction between the ocean and the wind blowing across its surface cause ocean surface currents. ______________

Match each definition with its term.

	Definition	Term
____	**2.** large whirl of water within an ocean basin	a. gyre
____	**3.** mass of ocean water that flows from place to place	b. upwelling
____	**4.** rising of cold, deep ocean water to replace warmer surface water	c. surface current
____	**5.** horizontal water movement in the upper part of the ocean's surface	d. ocean current

6. Select the appropriate letter on the map that identifies each of the following ocean currents.
 _____ North Atlantic Gyre
 _____ North Pacific Gyre
 _____ South Atlantic Gyre
 _____ South Pacific Gyre
 _____ Indian Ocean Gyre

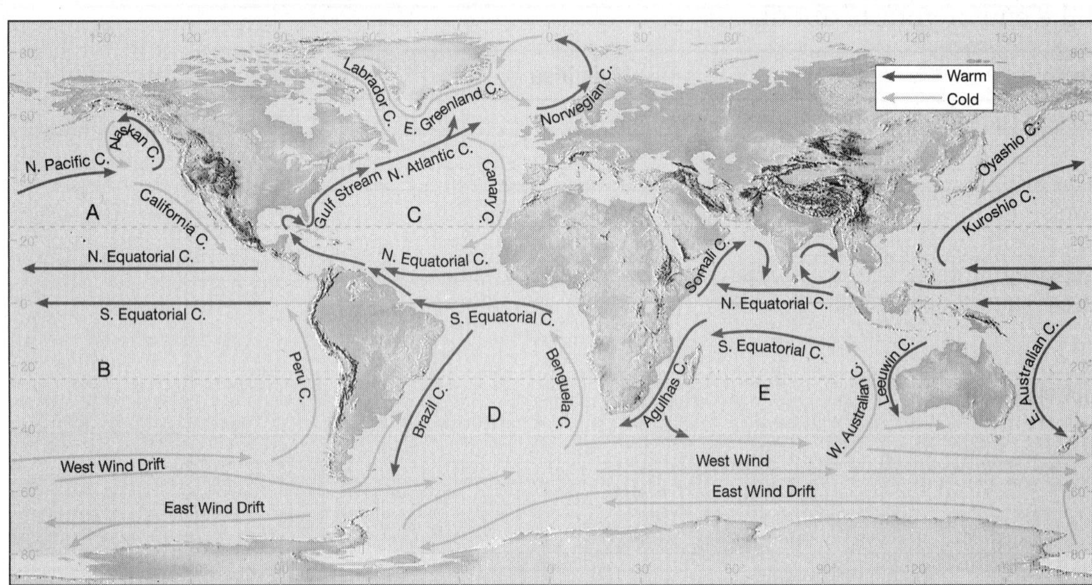

7. How does the Coriolis effect impact ocean currents in the Northern and Southern Hemispheres? ______________________________

____

____

8. Ocean currents moving from low-latitude to higher latitude regions transfer ________________ from warmer to cooler areas.

9. Is the following sentence true or false? Winds cause upwelling, which in turn causes an increase in dissolved nutrients at the ocean surface. ________________

Deep-Ocean Circulation

10. What are density currents? ______________________________

____

____

11. Ocean water can increase in density as a result of a decrease in temperature or a(n) ________________ in salinity.

12. Circle the letter of the area where the ocean water with the highest density occurs.
 a. at the equator b. near Antarctica
 c. in the Mediterranean Sea d. near Australia

Name _______________ Class _______________ Date _______________

Section 16.2 Waves and Tides

This section discusses waves and tides and explains what causes them.

Reading Strategy

Building Vocabulary As you read this section, define in your own words each vocabulary term listed in the table. For more information on this Reading Strategy, see the **Reading and Study Skills** in the **Skills and Reference Handbook** at the end of your textbook.

Vocabulary Term	Definition
Wave height	a.
Wavelength	b.
Wave period	c.
Fetch	d.

Waves

1. Waves in the ocean are _______________ traveling along the water.

2. Circle the letter of the source of most waves' energy and motion.
   a. Earth's gravity
   b. wind
   c. Earth's rotation
   d. the moon's gravity

3. The distance wind travels across open ocean water is called _______________.

4. What three factors determine the height, length, and period of ocean waves? _______________

5. Write the name of the wave part represented by each of the following letters in the figure.
   A. ____________________
   B. ____________________
   C. ____________________
   D. ____________________

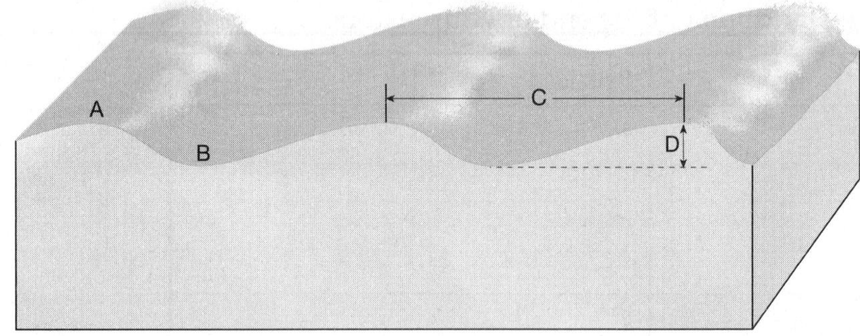

6. Is the following sentence true or false? Through circular orbital motion, wave energy moves forward through ocean water, while individual water particles move around in a circle, staying essentially in the same place. ____________________

Tides

7. What causes ocean tides? ____
____
____

8. Circle the letter of the force that produces tides.
   a. gravity
   b. wind
   c. pressure
   d. friction

9. Is the following sentence true or false? Most places on Earth experience one low tide and one high tide each day.
____

Match each definition with its term.

	Definition	Term
_____	10. tide with the greatest difference in height between successive high and low tides	a. spring tide
_____	11. tide with the least difference in height between successive high and low tides	b. neap tide
_____	12. difference in height between successive high and low tides	c. tidal range

13. Worldwide, the three main tidal patterns that exist are diurnal tides, ____________________ tides, and mixed tides.

Name ______________________ Class ________________ Date __________

Section 16.3 Shoreline Processes and Features

This section explains how forces acting upon the ocean shoreline impact it and create landforms.

Reading Strategy

Summarizing Complete the concept map to organize what you know about refraction. For more information on this Reading Strategy, see the **Reading and Study Skills** in the **Skills and Reference Handbook** at the end of your textbook.

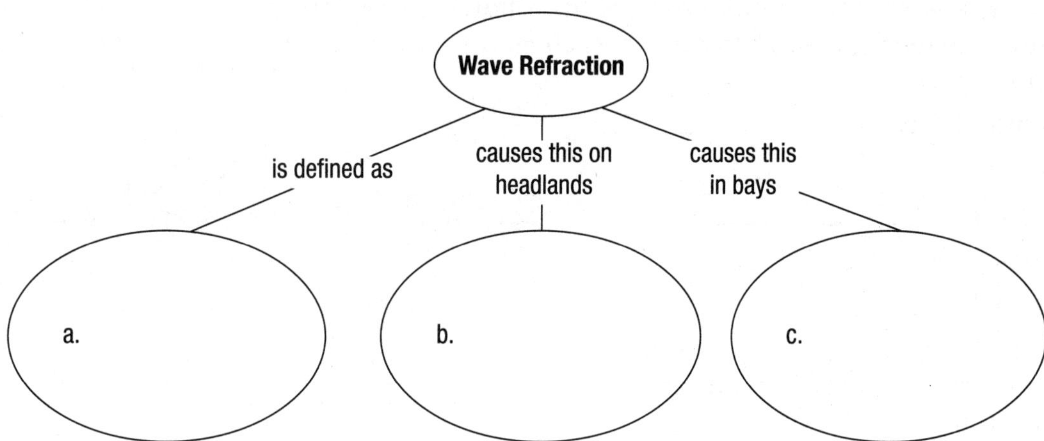

Forces Acting on the Shoreline

1. Is the following sentence true or false? Land features come and go along a shoreline because waves are constantly eroding, transporting, and depositing sediment there. ________________

2. Circle the letter of the sentence that is true about the result of wave refraction.
   a. Wave energy is concentrated in bays, causing erosion.
   b. Wave action is weakened in bays, causing erosion.
   c. Wave energy is concentrated at the end of headlands, causing erosion.
   d. Wave action is weakened at the end of headlands, causing deposition.

3. What are longshore currents? ______________________________________

____

____

4. In a surf zone, longshore currents are able to easily move sediment because the water there is ________________.

Name ______________________ Class ________________ Date ____________

Erosional Features

5. How are erosional and depositional features along a shoreline alike and different? ____

____

____

____

6. When two sea caves on opposite sides of a headland are eroded and unite, a(n) ________________ forms.

Depositional Features

7. Write the letter that identifies each of the following shoreline features in the figures. Then classify each feature as erosional or depositional.

baymouth bay ________________

spit ________________

sea stack ________________

wave-cut cliff ________________

tombolo ________________

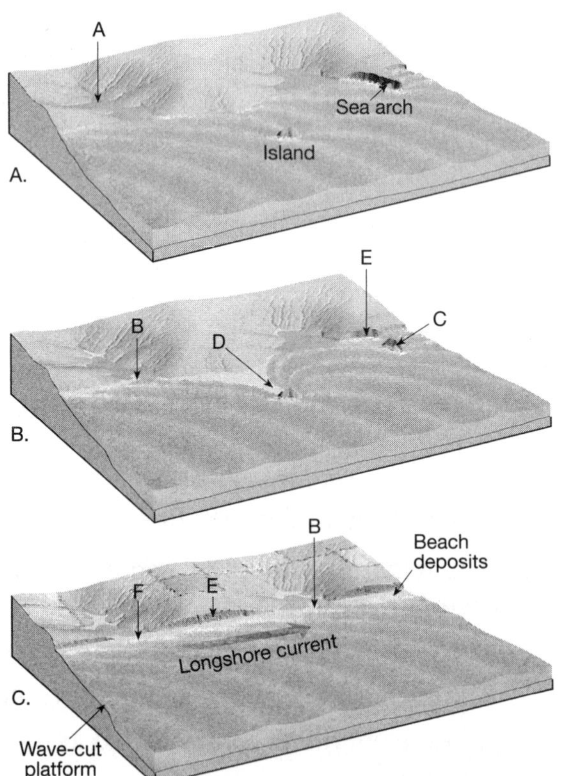

8. Circle the letter of a narrow sandbar that is parallel to but separate from a coastline.
   a. headland
   b. spit
   c. tombolo
   d. barrier island

Stabilizing the Shore

9. Is the following sentence true or false? Groins are barriers built at right angles to beaches to protect them from sediment deposition.

____

10. Circle the letter of a structure built parallel to a shore to shield it from breaking waves.
    a. breakwater
    b. spit
    c. seawall
    d. groin

11. The addition of large quantities of sand to the beach by people is called ________________.

Name ____________________ Class ________________ Date ___________

WordWise

Complete the sentences by using the scrambled vocabulary terms below.

eibarrr danissl	nigrsp deti
endyits cturrnse	awev tricerfona
upingllew	evaw eighth
reyg	gwtahvelen
coane urctenr	chetf
ahbce	ooiislrc eectff
ewav eprido	

The ____________________ is the deflection of ocean currents away from their original course as a result of Earth's rotation.

A(n) ____________________ has the greatest difference in height between successive high and low tides.

The accumulation of sediment found along the shore of a lake or an ocean is known as a(n) ____________________.

The rising of cold, deep ocean water to replace warmer surface water is known as ____________________.

The ____________________ is the time it takes one full wave to pass a fixed position.

The bending of waves, called ____________________, plays an important role in shoreline processes.

Vertical currents of ocean water that result from density differences among water masses are referred to as____________________.

A horizontal distance called ____________________ is measured between two successive wave crests or troughs.

Narrow sandbars, or____________________, are parallel to but separate from coastlines.

The vertical distance between a wave trough and a wave crest is the ____________________.

A large whirl of water within an ocean basin is a(n)____________________.

The distance wind travels across the open ocean is called ____________________.

A(n) ____________________ is a mass of ocean water that flows from one place to another.

Section 17.1 Atmosphere Characteristics

This section describes the components and vertical structure of the atmosphere. It also explains how the relationship between Earth and the sun causes the seasons.

Reading Strategy

Comparing and Contrasting As you read, complete the Venn diagram by comparing and contrasting summer and winter solstices. For more information on this Reading Strategy, see the **Reading and Study Skills** in the **Skills and Reference Handbook** at the end of your textbook.

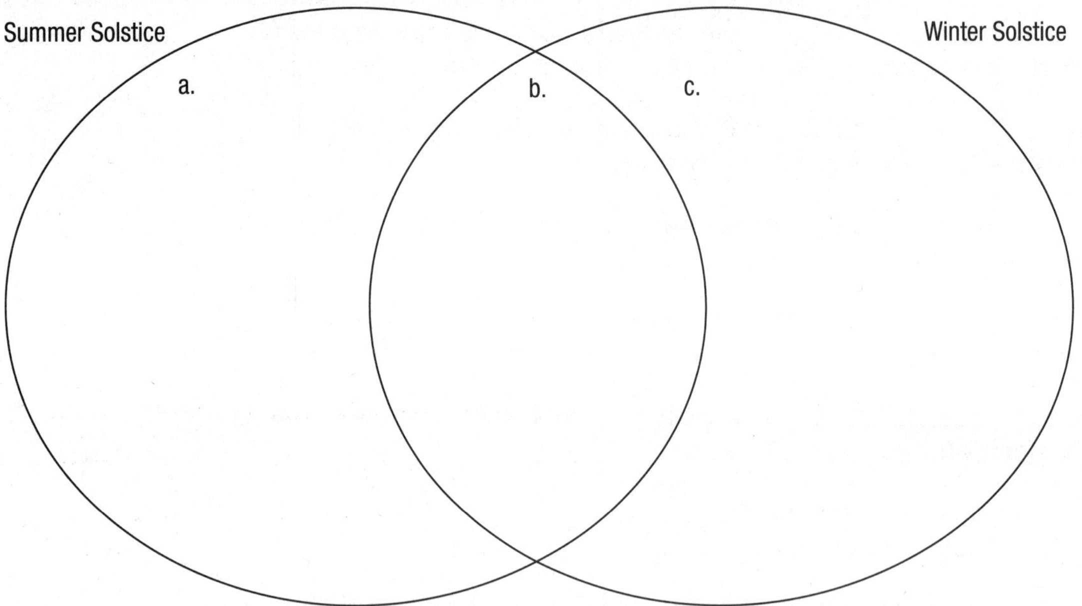

1. ______________ is the state of the atmosphere at any given time and place.

Composition of the Atmosphere

2. Circle the letter of the gas that is the largest component of the atmosphere.
   a. oxygen
   b. nitrogen
   c. water vapor
   d. carbon dioxide
3. Is the following sentence true or false? The source of all clouds and precipitation is water vapor. ______________
4. Why is the ozone layer crucial to life on Earth? ______________

Height and Structure of the Atmosphere

5. Is the following sentence true or false? Atmospheric pressure increases with height.
____

Name ______________________ Class ______________________ Date ______________

6. Select the appropriate letter in the figure that identifies each of the following layers of the atmosphere.

_____ mesosphere _____ thermosphere

_____ troposphere _____ stratosphere

7. In the figure, the atmosphere is divided vertically into four layers based on ______________________.

8. Circle the letter of the layer of the atmosphere that contains the ozone layer.

a. troposphere b. stratosphere

c. mesosphere d. thermosphere

Earth-Sun Relationships

9. What are Earth's two principal motions?

____

10. Select the appropriate letter in the figure that identifies each of the following months.

_____ March _____ December

_____ June _____ September

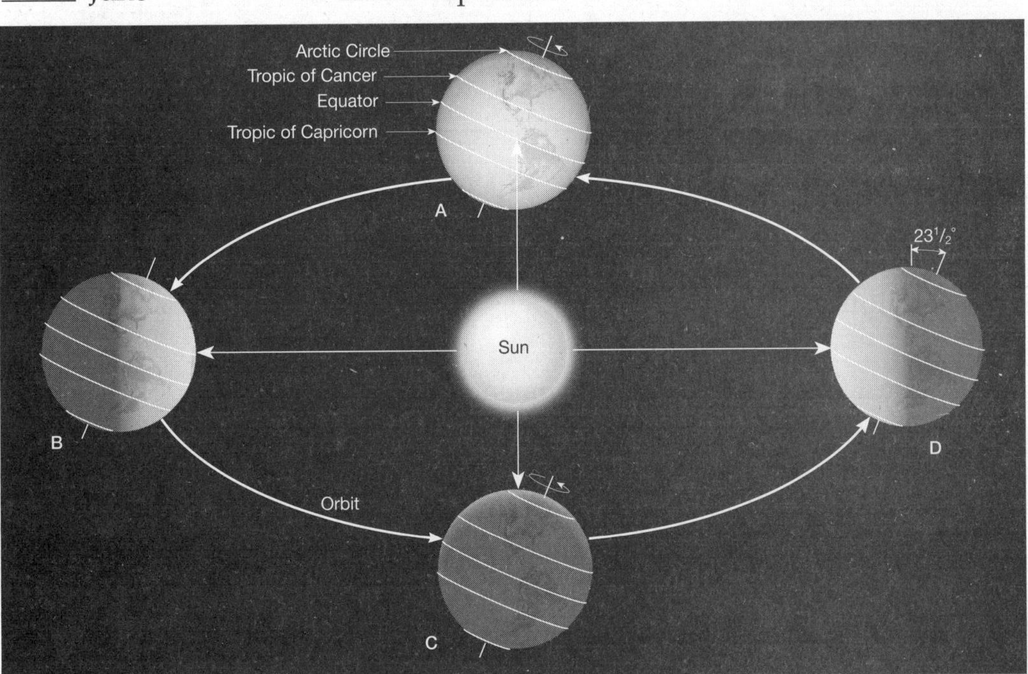

11. Is the following sentence true or false? At position B in the figure, the Northern Hemisphere will have longer daylight than darkness. ______________

12. What causes seasonal changes? ______________________________

____

____

Section 17.2 Heating the Atmosphere

This section describes the three ways in which heat can be transferred. It also explains what happens to solar radiation that hits Earth's atmosphere and surface.

Reading Strategy

Using Prior Knowledge Before you read, write your definition for each term. After you read, write the scientific definition of each term and compare it to your original definition. For more information on this Reading Strategy, see the **Reading and Study Skills** in the **Skills and Reference Handbook** at the end of your textbook.

Term	Your Definition	Scientific Definition
Heat		
Temperature		

Energy Transfer as Heat

Match each description with its mechanism of energy transfer.

	Description	Mechanism of Energy Transfer
_____	**1.** transfer of heat by mass movement or circulation within a substance	a. radiation
_____	**2.** transfer of heat through matter by molecular activity	b. convection
_____	**3.** transfer of heat without requiring a medium to travel through	c. conduction

4. Circle the letter of the act of light bouncing off an object.

a. absorption

b. scattering

c. reflection

d. radiation

Name ______________________ Class ______________________ Date ______________

5. Complete the chart below.

Mechanism of Energy Transfer		
Mechanism	**Requires direct contact?**	**Requires a medium?**
Conduction	yes	
Convection		
Radiation		

6. Is the following sentence true or false? All objects at any temperature emit radiant energy. ______________

7. Hotter objects emit ______________ total energy per unit area than colder objects do.

8. Is the following sentence true or false? The hotter a radiating body is, the longer the wavelengths of maximum radiation it will produce. ______________

9. Objects that are good absorbers of radiation are also good ______________ of radiation.

What Happens to Solar Radiation?

10. List three things that can happen when radiation strikes an object. ____

____

____

____

11. Circle the letter of the process that produces rays that travel in all directions.
   a. absorption
   b. transmission
   c. reflection
   d. scattering

12. About ______________ percent of the solar energy reaching the outer atmosphere is reflected or scattered back into space.

13. What is the greenhouse effect? ____

____

____

____

14. Is the following sentence true or false? Another term for the greenhouse effect is global warming. ______________

Name ______________ Class ______________ Date ______________

Section 17.3 Temperature Controls

This section describes the factors that influence temperature and discusses worldwide temperature distribution.

Reading Strategy

Previewing Before you read, use Figure 15 to describe the temperature variations for Vancouver and Winnipeg. For more information on this Reading Strategy, see the **Reading and Study Skills** in the **Skills and Reference Handbook** at the end of your textbook.

Temperature Variations	
Vancouver	
Winnipeg	

Why Temperatures Vary

1. List five factors other than latitude that exert a strong influence on temperature.

____

____

____

____

Match each location with its effect on temperature. You may use some effects more than once.

Location

_____ 2. windward of a large body of water

_____ 3. at a low altitude

_____ 4. on a leeward coast

_____ 5. behind a mountain range

_____ 6. at a high altitude

Effect on Temperature

a. lower temperatures

b. higher temperatures

c. more moderate temperatures

d. less moderate temperatures

7. Circle the letter of the sentence that is true.

a. Land heats more rapidly and cools more slowly than water.

b. Land heats more rapidly and cools more rapidly than water.

c. Land heats more slowly and cools more slowly than water.

d. Land heats more slowly and cools more rapidly than water.

Name ____________ Class ____________ Date ____________

8. Why does the Southern Hemisphere have smaller annual temperature variations than the Northern Hemisphere?

____

____

____

____

9. Is the following sentence true or false? A location on a windward coast will have a more moderate climate than an inland location at the same latitude. ____________

10. Mountains can affect temperatures by acting as ____________.

11. How does altitude affect mean temperature? ____________

____

____

____

12. Circle the letter of the correct definition of *albedo.*
   a. line that connects points with the same temperature
   b. fraction of total radiation reflected by a surface
   c. trapping of heat in Earth's atmosphere
   d. transfer of heat by movement within a substance

13. What effect do clouds have on incoming solar radiation? ____________

____

____

____

14. Is the following sentence true or false? Clouds have the same effect on temperatures during the night as they do during the day.

____

World Distribution of Temperature

15. Circle the letter of the lines on a map that connect points with the same temperature.
   a. albedos
   b. altitudes
   c. latitudes
   d. isotherms

16. What general trend does a world isothermal map show? ____________

____

____

____

Name ____________________ Class ________________ Date ____________

WordWise

Complete the sentences by using the scrambled vocabulary terms below.

oureenhgse cefetf	tinrwe etolssic	thae
stohopperre	msrtheiso	psorseheme
gsirnp oenuixq	lauaumtn nexuiqo	nzoeo
mtehrosperhe	rremeauettp	nsatecrigt
msmeur sscotile	oonuncctdi	elodba
oraiiatnd	pssratorhtee	vococentin

The ________________ is the bottom layer of the atmosphere.

Many clouds reflect a lot of sunlight because they have a high ________________.

Temperatures decrease in the third layer of the atmosphere, the ________________.

The ________________ contains only a tiny fraction of the atmosphere's mass.

The ________________ is the first day of summer.

In the Northern Hemisphere, the ________________ occurs on September 22 or 23.

________________ is a form of oxygen with three oxygen atoms in each molecule.

Solar energy reaches Earth by ________________.

March 21 or 22 is the ________________ in the Northern Hemisphere.

________________ is the energy transferred from one object to another due to a difference in their temperatures.

The average kinetic energy of the atoms or molecules in a substance is its ________________.

The ozone layer is found in the ________________.

When you touch a hot metal spoon, you experience heat transferred by ________________.

The lines on a world isothermal map are called ________________.

Water being heated in a pan circulates because of ________________.

Light reaches areas that are not in direct light by means of ________________.

Winter begins on the ________________.

The ________________ keeps Earth warm enough to be a suitable habitat for most living things.

Name ______________________ Class __________________ Date ____________

Section 18.1 Water in the Atmosphere

This section describes how water changes from one state to another. It also explains humidity and relative humidity.

Reading Strategy

In the table below, list what you know about water in the atmosphere and what you would like to learn. After you read, list what you have learned. For more information on this Reading Strategy, see the **Reading and Study Skills** in the **Skills and Reference Handbook** at the end of your textbook.

What I Know	What I Would Like to Learn	What I Have Learned
a.	b.	c.
d.	e.	f.

1. Circle the letter of the most important gas in atmospheric processes.
   a. oxygen b. nitrogen
   c. water vapor d. carbon dioxide

Water's Changes of State

2. Select the appropriate letter in the figure that identifies each of the following changes of state.
   _____ sublimation _____ freezing
   _____ deposition _____ evaporation
   _____ condensation _____ melting

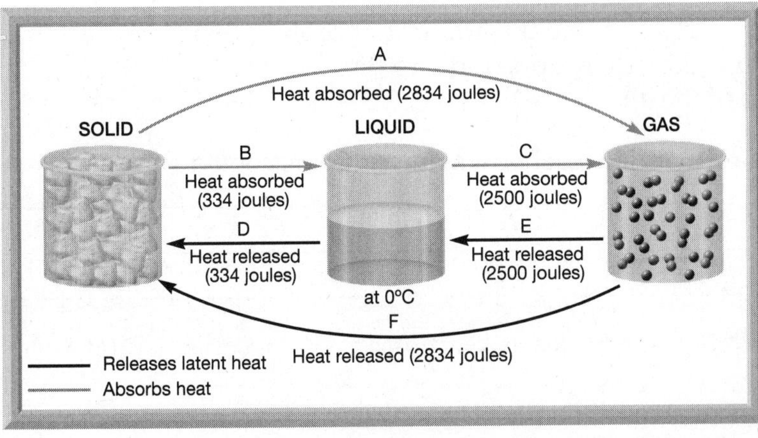

3. For each change of state, write the opposite change of state.
   a. condensation: ________________
   b. freezing: ________________
   c. deposition: ________________

4. The heat absorbed or released during a change of state is called ________________.

Humidity

5. Is the following sentence true or false? Saturated warm air contains more water vapor than saturated cold air.
   ____

6. What is the difference between humidity and relative humidity?
   ____
   ____
   ____
   ____

Match each situation to its change in relative humidity.

	Situation	Change in Relative Humidity
_____	7. Water vapor is added.	a. increases
_____	8. Air temperature decreases.	b. no change
_____	9. Water vapor is removed.	c. decreases
_____	10. Air temperature increases.	

11. When a parcel of air is cooled to the temperature at which it is saturated, it has reached its ________________.

12. Circle the letter of the factor that a hygrometer is used to measure.
    a. humidity
    b. relative humidity
    c. temperature
    d. latent heat

13. A sling psychrometer works because the amount of cooling that occurs in the wet bulb is directly proportional to the ________________ of the air.

14. What happens when air that has reached its dew point is cooled further? ________________________________
    ____
    ____

Name ______________________ Class ______________ Date ____________

Section 18.2 Cloud Formation

This section explains what happens when air is compressed and expanded. It also describes processes that lift air, how stable and unstable air behaves, and how condensation occurs.

Reading Strategy

As you read, write the main idea for each topic in the table below. For more information on this Reading Strategy, see the **Reading and Study Skills** in the **Skills and Reference Handbook** at the end of your textbook.

Topic	Main idea
Adiabatic temperature changes	a.
Stability measurements	b.
Degrees of stability	c.

Air Compression and Expansion

1. When a parcel of air is allowed to expand, it ______________.

2. Why does a parcel of air expand as it rises upward through the atmosphere?

____

____

3. Is the following sentence true or false? The rate of heating or cooling of saturated air is the dry adiabatic rate.

____

4. When a parcel of air reaches it dew point, the process of ______________ begins.

5. After a parcel of air rises past the condensation level, the rate of cooling decreases because of the release of latent ______________.

Processes That Lift Air

6. List four mechanisms that can cause air to rise.

____

____

7. Complete the table below.

Processes That Lift Air		
Process	**Cause of Lifting**	**Typical Resulting Weather Pattern**
Orographic lifting	mountains block airflow	
Frontal wedging		clouds and rain
Convergence		
Localized convective lifting		

8. What causes a rain shadow desert? ____
____
____
____

9. A(n) ____________________ is produced when two air masses collide.

10. Is the following sentence true or false? Localized convective lifting produces thermals that lift birds to great heights.
____

Stability

11. A parcel of air that is less dense than the surrounding air is ____________________ and will tend to rise.

12. Is the following sentence true or false? Unstable air tends to remain in its original position. ____________________

13. Circle the letter of the sentence that best describes a temperature inversion.
    a. Air temperature increases with height.
    b. Air temperature decreases with height.
    c. Low-altitude air is unstable.
    d. High-altitude air is unstable.

14. Clouds associated with lifting of ____________________ air often produce thunderstorms.

Condensation

15. For condensation to occur, air must be ____________________.

16. Is the following sentence true or false? Above the ground, tiny particles called condensation nuclei serve as surfaces for water-vapor condensation. ____________________

Section 18.3 Cloud Types and Precipitation

This section describes different types of clouds, including fog. It also explains how precipitation forms and describes different types of precipitation.

Reading Strategy

As you read, add definitions for the vocabulary terms. For more information on this Reading Strategy, see the **Reading and Study Skills** in the **Skills and Reference Handbook** at the end of your textbook.

Vocabulary Term	Definition
Cirrus	a.
Cumulus	b.
Stratus	c.
Coalescence	d.

Types of Clouds

1. Is the following sentence true or false? Clouds are classified based on form and height. _______________

2. The three types of _______________ clouds are cirrus, cirrostratus, and cirrocumulus.

3. Which photograph shows cumulus clouds? _____

4. Which photograph shows cirrus clouds? _____

A.

B.

5. How can you tell from the name of a cloud if it is a middle-range cloud?

____

____

____

6. Circle the letter of each cloud type that is a low cloud.
   a. stratus
   b. altostratus
   c. stratocumulus
   d. nimbostratus

Fog

7. Define *fog*. ____

____

____

8. Is the following sentence true or false? Fogs can be formed by cooling or by evaporation. ________________

How Precipitation Forms

9. What must happen for precipitation to form? ____________________

____

10. Formation of precipitation in cold clouds is called the ________________ process.

11. Is the following sentence true or false? In warm clouds, raindrops form by the Bergeron process. ________________

12. Circle the letter of the word that describes water in the liquid state below 0°C.
   a. supersaturated
   b. coalesced
   c. saturated
   d. supercooled

Forms of Precipitation

Match each description with its form of precipitation.

	Description	Form of Precipitation
_____	13. small particles of ice	a. hail
_____	14. drops of water that fall from a cloud and have a diameter of at least 0.5 mm	b. sleet
_____	15. ice pellets with multiple layers	c. rain

Name ______________________ Class ______________________ Date ______________

Section 19.1 Atmosphere Characteristics

This section explains what air pressure is and how it is measured. It also describes the factors that cause and control wind.

Reading Strategy

As you read, write the main ideas for each topic in the table. For more information on this Reading Strategy, see the **Reading and Study Skills** in the **Skills and Reference Handbook** at the end of your textbook.

Topic	Main Ideas
Air Pressure Defined	Air pressure is the weight of air above. It is exerted in all directions.
Measuring Air Pressure	a.
Factors Affecting Wind	b.

Air Pressure Defined

1. Air pressure is the pressure exerted by the ______________________ of air above a certain point.

2. Why doesn't the weight of air above a table crush it? ______________________

____

____

____

3. Is the following sentence true or false? Average air pressure is about the same as that produced by a column of water 10 m high. ______________________

Measuring Air Pressure

4. Circle the letter of the instrument used to measure air pressure.

   a. thermometer

   b. barometer

   c. anemometer

   d. aneroidometer

5. When air pressure increases, the mercury in the tube of a mercury barometer ________________.

6. Is the following sentence true or false? The mercury barometer was invented by Galileo. ________________

7. List two advantages of the aneroid barometer over the mercury barometer. ____

____

____

Factors Affecting Wind

8. Wind is caused by horizontal differences in ________________.

9. Is the following sentence true or false? Pressure differences that cause wind are generated by unequal heating of Earth's surface. ________________

10. What three factors combine to control wind? ____

____

11. How are isobars related to pressure gradients? ____

____

____

12. Due to the Coriolis effect, winds in the Northern Hemisphere are deflected to the ________________.

13. Is the following sentence true or false? The Coriolis effect occurs because Earth rotates underneath the path of moving objects. ________________

14. How does friction affect wind? ____

____

15. ________________ are high-altitude fast-moving rivers of air that travel from west to east.

16. Complete the table below.

Factors That Affect Wind		
Factor	**Ultimate Cause**	**Effect on Wind**
Pressure Differences	unequal heating of Earth's surface by the sun	
Coriolis Effect		
Friction		

Name ______________________ Class ______________ Date __________

Section 19.2 Pressure Centers and Winds

This section describes cyclones, anticyclones, and global wind patterns.

Reading Strategy

As you read about pressure centers and winds, complete the table indicating to which hemisphere the concept applies. Use *N* for Northern Hemisphere, *S* for Southern Hemisphere, or *B* for both. For more information on this Reading Strategy, see the **Reading and Study Skills** in the **Skills and Reference Handbook** at the end of your textbook.

Cyclones rotate counterclockwise.	a.
Net flow of air is inward around a cyclone.	b.
Anticyclones rotate counterclockwise.	c.
Coriolis effect deflects winds to the right.	d.

Highs and Lows

1. Cyclones are centers of ______________ pressure associated with clouds and precipitation.

2. Is the following sentence true or false? In an anticyclone, the value of the isobars increases from the center to the outside.

   ____

3. List the factors that cause winds in the Northern Hemisphere to blow inwards and counterclockwise around lows.

   ____

4. Is the following sentence true or false? In the Southern Hemisphere, winds around a cyclone flow outward.

   ____

5. These figures show side views of the air movement in a high and low. Select the letter of the figure that identifies each of the following air movements.

   _____ surface low

   _____ divergence aloft

   _____ surface high

   _____ surface divergence

   _____ calm, clear weather

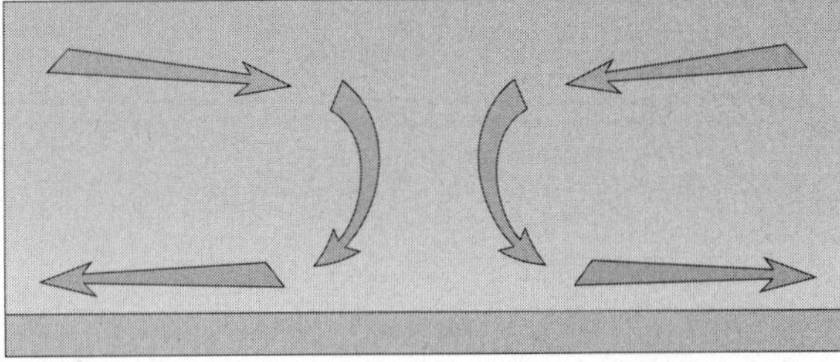

A.

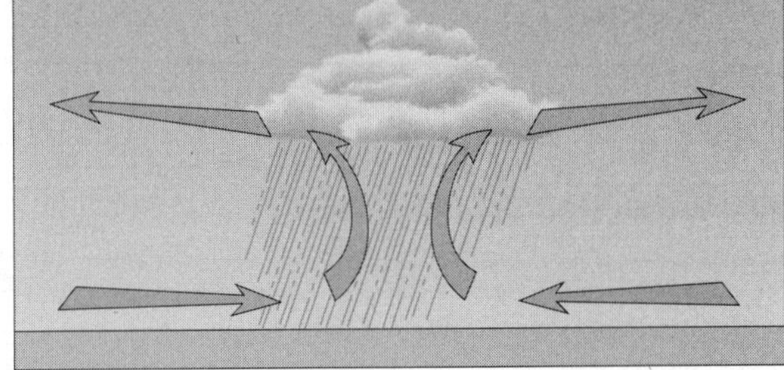

B.

6. Why do weather reports always emphasize cyclones and anticyclones? ____________

____

Global Winds

7. How does the atmosphere balance the amounts of energy received at different parts of Earth's surface?

____

____

____

8. Is the following sentence true or false? Earth's rotation causes the two-cell convection system to break down into smaller cells.

____

9. Select the appropriate letter in the figure that identifies each part of the global circulation model.

_____ NE trade winds

_____ polar easterlies

_____ equatorial low

_____ westerlies

_____ subtropical high

_____ SE trade winds

_____ subpolar low

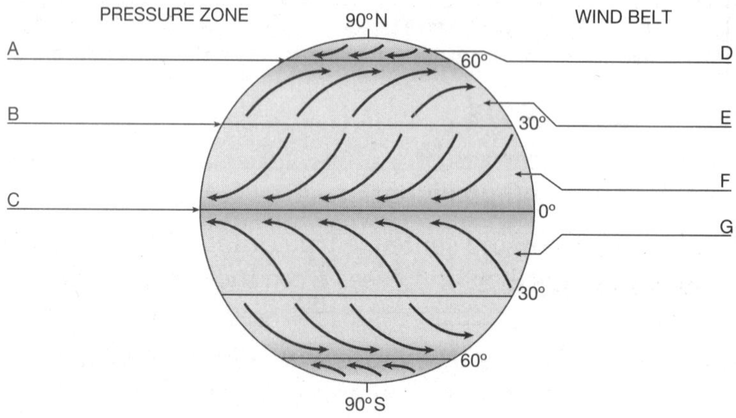

10. In which zone in the figure does sinking dry air produce deserts in some areas? ____________

11. Circle the letter of the winds near the equator that blow from easterly directions.

a. jet streams
b. westerlies
c. trade winds
d. polar easterlies

12. The interaction of westerlies and polar easterlies produces the ____________.

13. Is the following sentence true or false? Inward and upward airflow at the equatorial zone is associated with clouds and precipitation.

____

14. In North America, seasonal temperature differences over ____________ disrupt the global pressure pattern.

15. What causes monsoons? ____________

____

Name ______________________ Class ______________________ Date ______________

Section 19.3 Regional Wind Systems

This section discusses local winds and how wind is measured. It also explains El Niño and La Niña.

Reading Strategy

Before you read, use Figure 17 on page 547 to locate examples of the driest and wettest regions of Earth. After you read, identify the dominant wind system for each location. For more information on this Reading Strategy, see the **Reading and Study Skills** in the **Skills and Reference Handbook** at the end of your textbook.

Precipitation	Location	Dominant Wind System
Extremely low	a.	b.
Extremely high	c.	d.

Local Winds

1. ______________ are small-scale winds produced by a locally generated pressure gradient.

2. List two causes of local winds. ______________________________

____

Match each description with its local wind.

	Description	Local Wind
_____	3. During the day, heated air along mountain slopes rises.	a. land breeze
_____	4. During the day, heated air over land rises, allowing cooler air to move in from over water.	b. sea breeze
_____	5. At night, air over land cools and moves out over water.	c. valley breeze
_____	6. At night, cooled air along mountain slopes moves downward.	d. mountain breeze

7. Circle the letter of the locations where the coldest air pockets usually can be found.
   a. valley floors
   b. mountain peaks
   c. mountainsides
   d. plains

Name ______________________ Class ________________ Date __________

8. Does the figure show a land breeze or a sea breeze? Explain your answer. ____

____

____

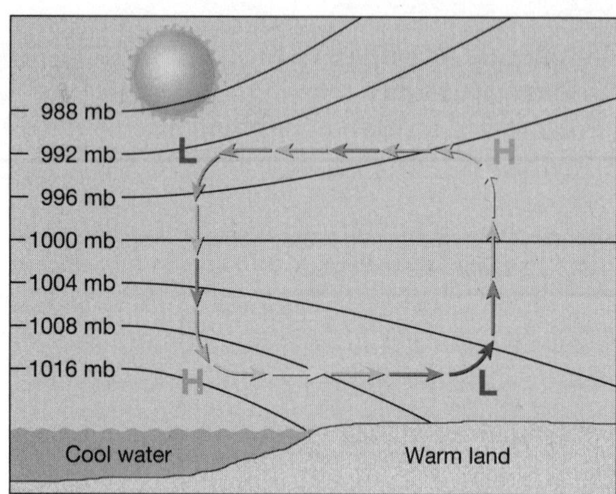

How Wind Is Measured

9. What is a prevailing wind? ____

____

____

10. In the United States, the ________________ move weather from west to east.

11. Circle the letter of the instrument used to measure wind speed.

a. thermometer b. barometer

c. anemometer d. wind vane

El Niño and La Niña

12. An episode of ocean warming that affects the eastern tropical Pacific is called ________________.

13. Is the following sentence true or false? El Niño episodes occur at irregular intervals of 3 to 7 years. ________________

14. What conditions trigger a La Niña episode? ____

____

____

Global Distribution of Precipitation

15. How are rain forests related to wind patterns? ____

____

____

16. Is the following sentence true or false? Areas dominated by subtropical low-pressure cells are often deserts. ________________

Name ______________________ Class __________________ Date ____________

Chapter 19 Air Pressure and Wind

WordWise

Use the clues below to identify vocabulary terms from Chapter 19. Write the terms, putting one letter in each blank. Use the circled letters to find the hidden word.

Clues

1. pressure exerted by the weight of air above a certain point
2. pressure changes occurring over a given distance
3. device used to measure air pressure
4. change in movement of winds resulting from Earth's rotation
5. center of low air pressure
6. stormy belt where westerlies encounter polar easterlies
7. seasonal change in wind direction due to summer heating of landmasses
8. easterly wind belts on either side of the equator
9. prevailing winds of the middle latitudes

Vocabulary Terms

1. ◯ _ _   _ _ _ _ _ _ _ _
2. _ _ _ _ _ _ _ _   _ _ _ _ _ _ ◯ _
3. _ _ _ _ _ _ ◯ _ _
4. _ _ _ ◯ _ _ _ _   _ _ _ _ _ _
5. ◯ ◯ ◯ _ _ _ _
6. _ _ ◯ _ _   _ _ _ _ _
7. _ _ _ _ _ ◯ _
8. _ _ _ _ _   _ _ ◯ _ _
9. _ _ _ _ _ _ _ _ ◯ _

Hidden Word: _ _ _ _ _ _ _ _ _ _ _

Definition: ____

Section 20.1 Air Masses

This section describes air masses and explains how they affect weather.

Reading Strategy

As you read, write a definition for each of the terms in the table. Refer to the table as you read the rest of the chapter. For more information on this Reading Strategy, see the **Reading and Study Skills** in the **Skills and Reference Handbook** at the end of your textbook.

Term	Definition
Air mass	a.
Source region	b.
Polar air mass	c.
Tropical air mass	d.
Continental air mass	e.
Maritime air mass	f.

Air Masses and Weather

1. Changes in weather patterns are often caused by movement of ______________.

2. Is the following sentence true or false? As an air mass moves, its characteristics change. ______________

3. Circle the letter of a common size for an air mass.
   a. 600 km or less across
   b. 1600 km or more across
   c. 16,000 km or more across
   d. 160,000 km or more across

Name ______________________ Class ______________ Date __________

Classifying Air Masses

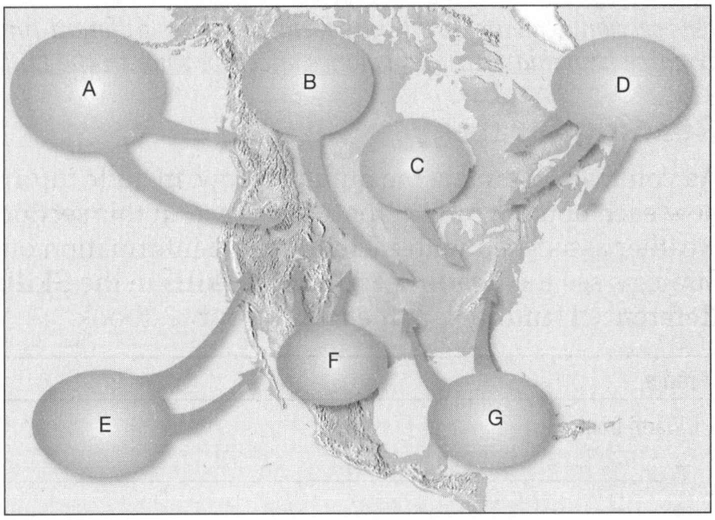

4. Identify each labeled air mass on the figure as continental tropical, continental polar, maritime polar, or maritime tropical.

A. ______________

B. ______________

C. ______________

D. ______________

E. ______________

F. ______________

G. ______________

5. List two characteristics used to classify air masses. ______________

6. Circle the letter of the terms that describe the temperature characteristics of an air mass.

a. continental and maritime
b. continental and tropical
c. polar and maritime
d. polar and tropical

Weather in North America

7. Is the following sentence true or false? Much of the weather in eastern North America is influenced by continental tropical and maritime polar air masses. ______________

8. Although ______________ air masses are not usually associated with heavy precipitation, they can sometimes cause lake-effect snow.

9. Circle the letter of the type of air mass that is the source of much of the precipitation that falls on the eastern United States.

a. continental tropical
b. maritime tropical
c. maritime polar
d. continental polar

10. Is the following sentence true or false? In the winter, maritime polar air masses often bring rain and snow to the west coast of North America. ______________

11. What causes Indian summer? ______________

Name ______________________ Class ________________ Date ____________

Section 20.2 Fronts

This section explains how fronts form, describes different types of fronts, and explains how mid-latitude cyclones affect weather in the United States.

Reading Strategy

As you read, complete the outline below. Include information about how each of the weather fronts discussed in this section forms and the weather associated with each. For more information on this Reading Strategy, see the **Reading and Study Skills** in the **Skills and Reference Handbook** at the end of your textbook.

Fronts
I. Warm front
A. ______________________________
B. ______________________________
II. Cold front
A. ______________________________
B. ______________________________
____
____
____
____
____
____

Formation of Fronts

1. A front is a(n) ________________ that separates two air masses.
2. Is the following sentence true or false? Like air masses, most fronts are very large. ________________

Types of Fronts

Match each description with its front.

	Description	Front
_____	3. Air flow is almost parallel to the line of the front, and the position of the front does not move.	a. warm front
_____	4. Cold, dense air moves into a region occupied by warmer air.	b. cold front
_____	5. Warm air moves into an area formerly covered by cooler air.	c. stationary front
_____	6. A cold front overtakes a warm front.	d. occluded front

7. A warm front often produces a(n) ________________ increase in temperature.

8. Is the following sentence true or false? Forceful lifting of air along a cold front can lead to heavy rain and strong winds.

____

Middle-Latitude Cyclones

9. The middle-latitude cyclone shown in the figure is a center of low ________________.

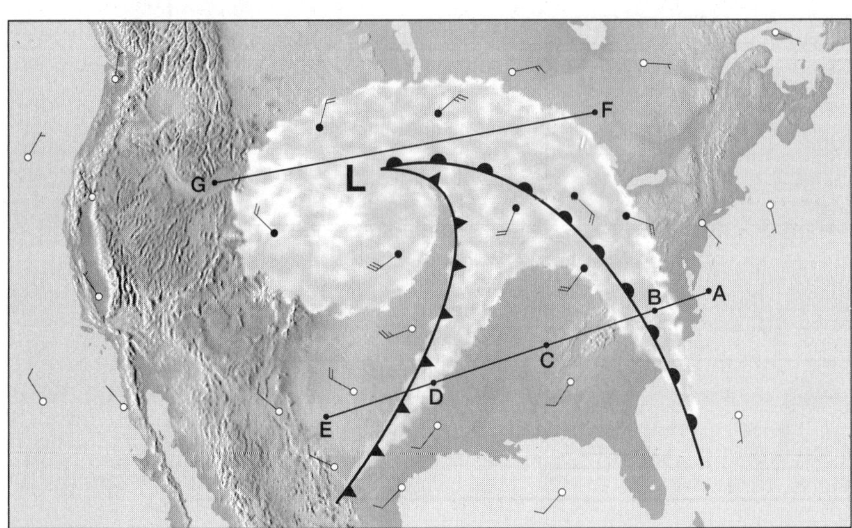

10. Name the type of front shown at each of these locations in the figure.

location B: ________________

location D: ________________

The Role of Airflow Aloft

11. What often fuels a middle-latitude cyclone? ________________________________

____

12. In what order do the stages of a middle-latitude cyclone shown in the figures occur? ________________

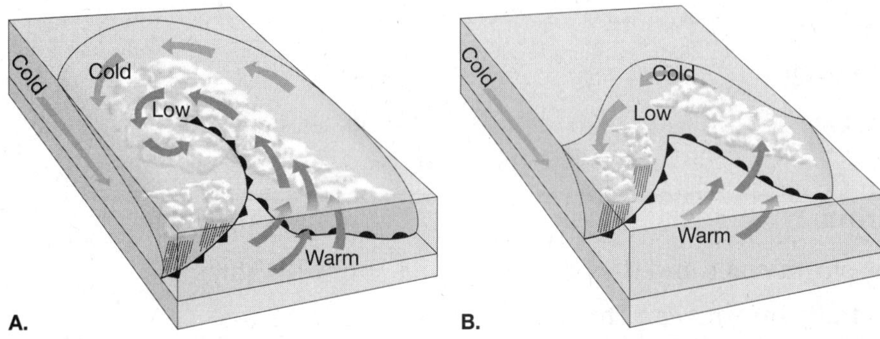

13. Is the following sentence true or false? Figure A shows the development of a stationary front. ________________

Name ______________________ Class ________________ Date ____________

Section 20.3 Severe Storms

This section discusses the causes and nature of thunderstorms, tornadoes, and hurricanes.

Reading Strategy

Complete the table as you read this section. For more information on this Reading Strategy, see the **Reading and Study Skills** in the **Skills and Reference Handbook** at the end of your textbook.

Severe Storms		
	Causes	**Effects**
Thunderstorms	a.	b.
Tornadoes	c.	d.
Hurricanes	e.	f.

Thunderstorms

1. A thunderstorm generates ______________ and thunder.

2. How do thunderstorms form? ______________________________

____

Using the figure, match each description to its thunderstorm stage.

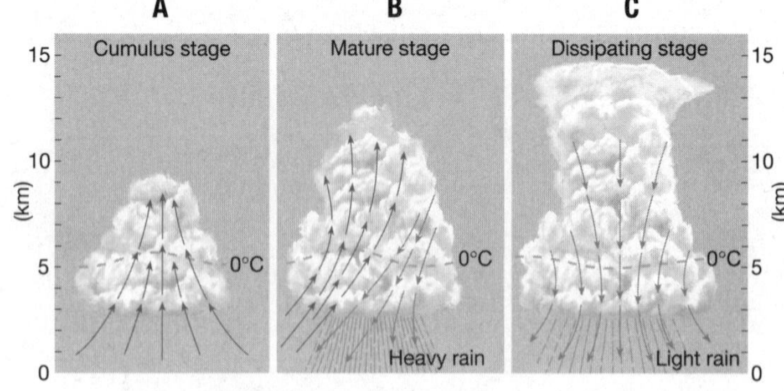

	Description	**Thunderstorm Stage**
_____	3. The storm cools and dies down.	a. cumulus stage
_____	4. Updrafts of warm air cause the cloud to grow upward.	b. mature stage
_____	5. Heavy precipitation falls.	c. dissipating stage

Tornadoes

6. A tornado is a violent windstorm in the form of a(n) ____________________ column of air.

7. Is the following sentence true or false? Tornadoes occur mainly in the winter. ____________________

8. Circle the letter of the type of storm usually associated with tornadoes.
   a. hurricane
   b. thunderstorm
   c. lake-effect snow
   d. typhoon

9. Why are the maximum winds inside a tornado so high? ____________________
   ____
   ____

10. A tornado ____________________ is issued when a tornado has actually been sighted in an area.

Hurricanes

11. To be considered a hurricane, a tropical ____________________ must produce sustained winds of at least 119 km per hour.

12. Is the following sentence true or false? Hurricanes are the most powerful storms on Earth. ____________________

13. Why are hurricanes becoming a growing threat? ____________________
   ____
   ____

14. Hurricanes usually develop in late summer because they are fueled by heat and moisture from ____________________ water.

15. Is the following sentence true or false? The greatest wind speeds and heaviest rainfall in a hurricane occur in the eye.
   ____

16. Circle the letter of the center of a hurricane.
   a. typhoon
   b. eye wall
   c. eye
   d. surge

17. When a hurricane's eye lands, a dome of water about 65 to 80 km wide called a ____________________ sweeps across the coast.

18. List two situations in which a hurricane weakens. ____________________
   ____
   ____

Name ____________________ Class ________________ Date ____________

Chapter 21 Climate

Section 21.1 Factors That Affect Climate

This section explains how latitude, elevation, topography, water, winds, and vegetation affect climate.

Reading Strategy

Summarizing Information As you read, summarize the effect(s) each factor has on climate. For more information on this Reading Strategy, see the **Reading and Study Skills** in the **Skills and Reference Handbook** at the end of your textbook.

Factor	Effect(s) on Climate
1. Latitude	a.
2. Elevation	b.
3. Topography	c.
4. Water bodies	d.
5. Global wind	e.
6. Vegetation	f.

Factors That Affect Climate

1. Circle the letter of the answer that correctly completes the following sentence. As latitude increases, the average intensity of solar energy

a. decreases. b. increases.

c. stays the same. d. is unrelated.

2. Temperate zones have ________________ summers and ________________ winters because of the angle of the sun's rays and the length of daylight in the summer and winter.

3. Why do the polar zones have cold temperatures year-round?

____

____

____

4. Is the following sentence true or false? The polar zones are located between 66.5° north and south latitudes and the poles.

____

5. Circle the letter of the region between the Tropic of Cancer and the Tropic of Capricorn.

a. polar zone b. temperate zone

c. tropics d. equator

6. What effect does elevation have on precipitation? ______________________________
____

7. Describe why a rain shadow occurs. ______________________________
____
____

8. Is the following sentence true or false? The higher the elevation is, the colder the climate. ______________

9. Circle the letter of the angle at which the sun's rays strike the surface of Earth in the tropics.
   a. almost a 45° angle
   b. almost a right angle
   c. less than a 45° angle
   d. more than a right angle

10. The figure below shows the rain shadow effect. Identify the labeled items on the lines provided.

a. ______________
b. ______________
c. ______________
d. ______________

Match each sentence with the term that completes it.

	Sentence	Term
_____	11. In the temperate zones, the sun's rays strike the Earth at a _________ angle than near the equator.	a. global winds
_____	12. When the sun's rays strike Earth at an angle less than 90°, the energy is spread out over a __________ area.	b. larger
_____	13. _______ distribute(s) heat and moisture around Earth.	c. precipitation
_____	14. Plants influence _________ through transpiration, which releases water vapor from their leaves into the air.	d. smaller

Section 21.2 World Climates

This section discusses the Köppen climate classification system and the various types of climates in the world.

Reading Strategy

Outlining As you read, complete the outline for each climate type discussed in this section. Include temperature and precipitation information for each climate type, as well as at least one location with that climate type. For more information on this Reading Strategy, see the **Reading and Study Skills** in the **Skills and Reference Handbook** at the end of your textbook.

I. World Climates
  A. Humid Tropical
    1. Wet tropics
    2. ______________________
  B. Humid mid-latitude
    1. ______________________
    2. ______________________
  C. Dry
    1. ______________________
    2. ______________________

The Köppen Climate Classification System

1. The Köppen climate classification system uses ________________ and annual values of ________________ and precipitation to classify climates.

2. Circle the letter of the climate that is NOT one of the principal groups in the Köppen system.
   a. humid tropical   b. dry
   c. humid mid-latitude   d. wet

Humid Tropical Climates

3. Humid tropical climates are climates without ________________.

4. What are the characteristics of a wet tropical climate? ______________________
____
____

5. Is the following sentence true or false? Tropical wet and dry climates have temperatures and total precipitation similar to those in the wet tropics, but experience distinct periods of low precipitation. ________________

Name ____________________ Class ____________________ Date ____________

Humid Mid-Latitude Climates

6. Describe mild and severe winters in the humid mid-latitude climates.

____

____

____

7. Circle the letters of the three types of climates that are classified as humid mid-latitude with mild winters.

   a. humid subtropical
   b. subarctic
   c. marine west coast
   d. dry-summer subtropical

8. Use the climate diagram for St. Louis, Missouri, on the right to answer the following questions.

   a. During which month does the highest temperature occur? What is the highest temperature? ____________

   b. During which month does the lowest temperature occur? What is the lowest temperature? ____________

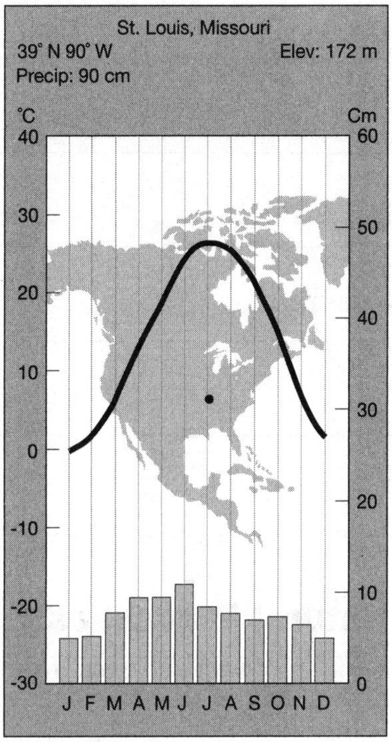

Dry Climates

9. Describe a dry climate and list the two types.

____

____

____

____

____

____

Polar Climates

10. Is the following sentence true or false? Polar climates are those in which the mean temperature of the warmest month is above 10°C. ____________

11. Circle the letters of the two types of polar climates.

   a. humid subtropical
   b. tundra
   c. Antarctic
   d. ice cap

Highland Climates

12. Describe highland climates. ____________________________________

____

____

____

____

Name ______________________ Class ________________ Date ____________

Chapter 21 Climate

Section 21.3 Climate Changes

This section describes natural processes and human activities that affect climate.

Reading Strategy

Identifying Cause and Effect As you read, complete the table below. For more information on this Reading Strategy, see the **Reading and Study Skills** in the **Skills and Reference Handbook** at the end of your textbook.

Climate Changes	
Causes	**Effects**

Natural Processes That Change Climate

1. How do aerosols from volcanic eruptions affect climate? ______________________________
____
____
____

2. Is the following sentence true or false? El Niño or a change in ocean circulation can result in short-term climate fluctuations.
____

3. The formation of sunspots appears to correspond with ________________ periods in Europe and North America.

4. Circle the letter of the motions of Earth that result in climatic changes.
   a. rotations
   b. plate tectonics
   c. changes in the shape of Earth's orbit
   d. ocean waves

Human Impact on Climate Changes

5. Circle the letter of the term for the natural warming of both Earth's lower atmosphere and Earth's surface.
   a. greenhouse effect
   b. tropical warming
   c. transpiration
   d. polar thawing

6. The major gases involved in the greenhouse effect are ________________ and ________________.

7. Explain why greenhouse gases are important for life on Earth.
____
____
____
____
____

8. Is the following sentence true or false? The burning of fossil fuels and the clearing of forests may have added to an increase of oxygen in the atmosphere. ________________

9. Use the graph below to answer the following questions.

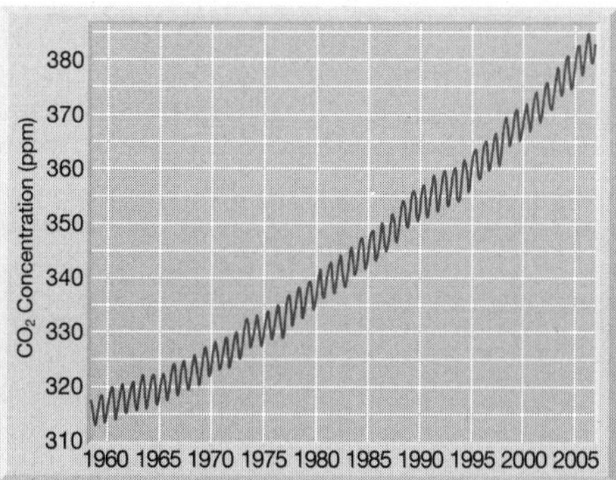

   a. What was the approximate concentration of carbon dioxide in the atmosphere in 1960? ________________
   b. What was the approximate concentration of carbon dioxide in the atmosphere in 2007? ________________
   c. What is the approximate difference in carbon dioxide concentration between 2007 and 1960? ________________

10. What is global warming? ____
____
____
____
____

Name ____________________ Class ________________ Date ____________

WordWise

Solve the clues to determine which vocabulary terms from Chapter 21 are hidden in the puzzle. Then find and circle the terms in the puzzle. The terms may occur vertically, horizontally, or diagonally.

```
T I N Z W L Z V L W S L I M
G E N E L R F I E K A V D O
N X M A P C V S F C B I H P
I G C P D P T Q I R M S B S
M V M K E C O P X U Q C L U
R E R Q O R O K H D K G K B
A E T A K R A P J Y M K R A
W T S L T M I T O S Y M A R
L T U B Z F P A E D V W L C
A B U S L A C I P O R T O T
B S C H M N A F W B K B P I
O P N G R E E N H O U S E C
L J G T Y S S I O T C V L J
G U R L B U K L X A V T Z W
```

Clues

The ________________ zone is a region that experiences warm weather year-round.

The natural warming of both Earth's lower atmosphere and Earth's surface is the ________________ effect.

The region located north of the humid continental climate and south of the tundra has a ________________ climate.

The ________________ climate classification system uses mean monthly and annual values of temperature and precipitation.

The increase of global temperatures due to increased levels of greenhouse gases is known as ________________.

The ________________ zone is a region that experiences hot summers and cold winters.

The dry-summer ________________ climate is sometimes referred to as a Mediterranean climate.

Coastal areas between about 40° and 65° north and south latitude have marine ________________ climates.

The southeastern United States has a ________________ subtropical climate.

The ________________ zone is a region that experiences very cold temperatures year-round.

Section 22.1 Early Astronomy

This section outlines the early history of astronomy, especially changing ideas about Earth's place in the universe.

Reading Strategy

As you read about the geocentric and heliocentric models of the solar system, complete the table. For more information on this Reading Strategy, see the **Reading and Study Skills** in the **Skills and Reference Handbook** at the end of your textbook.

	Location of Earth	Location of Sun	Supporters of Model
Geocentric Model	center of universe	a.	b.
Heliocentric Model	c.	d.	e.

Ancient Greeks

1. The study of the properties of objects in space and the laws under which the universe operates is called ________________.

2. Is the following sentence true or false? Eratosthenes is considered to be the first person to calculate the size of Earth. ________________

3. The idea that the moon, sun, and known planets orbit Earth is called the ________________ model of the universe.

4. Describe the heliocentric model of the universe. ____

5. Circle the letter of the statement that is true.
   a. The geocentric theory is correct.
   b. The geocentric theory is flawed and was immediately rejected.
   c. The geocentric theory is flawed but was accepted for thousands of years.
   d. The geocentric theory is accepted today.

6. The figure shows the apparent motion of Mars as seen from Earth. What type of motion is occurring between points 3 and 4?

____

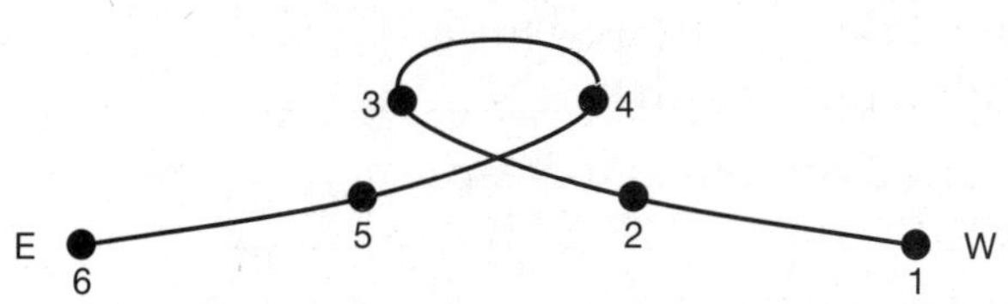

7. Is the following sentence true or false? Ptolemy's geocentric model was unable to account for the observed retrograde motion of the planets. ________________

The Birth of Modern Astronomy

Match each description with its astronomer.

Description	Astronomer
_____ 8. developed a model of the solar system with the sun at the center	a. Johannes Kepler
_____ 9. formulated and tested the law of universal gravitation	b. Isaac Newton
_____ 10. discovered three laws of planetary motion	c. Galileo Galilei
_____ 11. made much more precise observations than previous astronomers made	d. Nicolaus Copernicus
_____ 12. described the behavior of moving objects	e. Tycho Brahe

13. Circle the letter of the word that describes the shape of the planet's orbit as shown in the figure.

a. circle b. retrograde c. ellipse d. focus

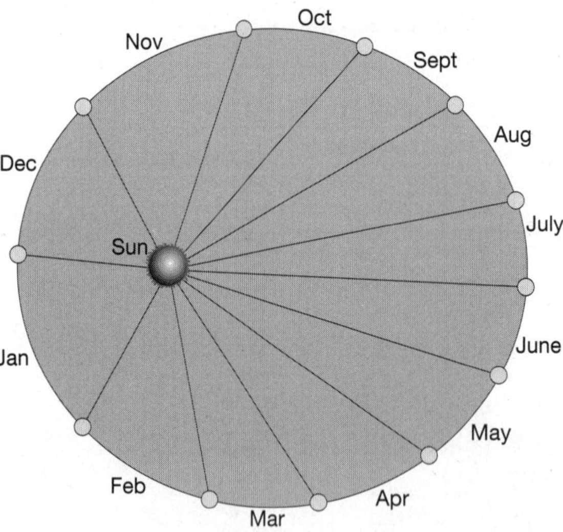

14. Is the following sentence true or false? During December and January on the figure, the planet is moving the fastest.

____

15. If the planet in the figure is Earth, the average distance from the planet to the sun is about 150 million km, or one ________________.

16. List the two factors that Newton showed combined to keep the planets in their elliptical orbits. ________________________________

____

Name ______________________ Class ________________ Date ____________

Section 22.2 The Earth-Moon-Sun System

This section describes how Earth moves in space and how changes in the relative positions of Earth, the sun, and the moon cause seasons, phases of the moon, and eclipses.

Reading Strategy

As you read, complete the flowchart to show how eclipses occur. For more information on this Reading Strategy, see the **Reading and Study Skills** in the **Skills and Reference Handbook** at the end of your textbook.

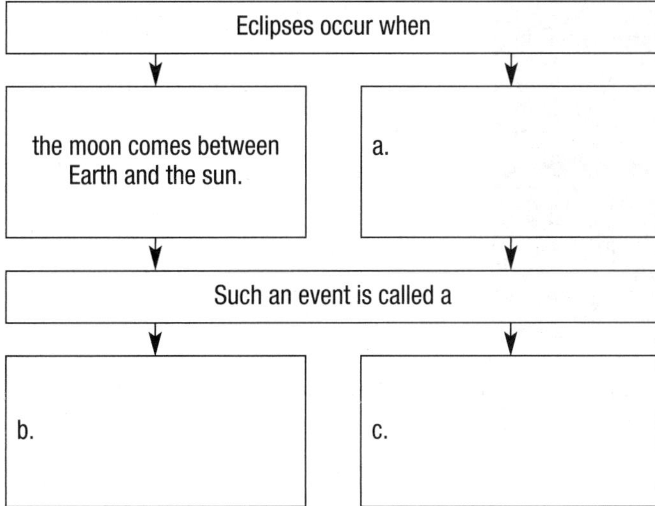

Motions of Earth

1. Circle the letter of the two main motions of Earth.
   a. rotation and precession b. rotation and revolution
   c. revolution and precession d. rotation and aphelion

2. Is the following sentence true or false? Day and night are caused by Earth's revolution on its axis. ________________

3. The point at which Earth is closest to the sun is called ________________.

4. Is the following sentence true or false? Seasons are caused in part by the tilt of Earth's axis of rotation. ________________

5. What is precession? ____

____

Motions of the Earth-Moon System

6. Circle the letter of the term that describes the point at which the moon is farthest from Earth.
   a. apogee b. aphelion c. perigee d. perihelion

7. Identify each labeled phase on the figure as one of the following: waning gibbous, first quarter, waning crescent, waxing gibbous, new, waxing crescent, full, third quarter.

1. ________________ 4. ________________ 7. ________________
2. ________________ 5. ________________ 8. ________________
3. ________________ 6. ________________

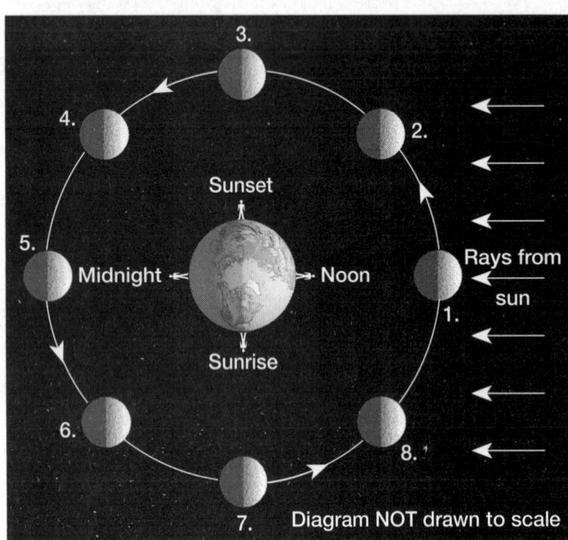

8. Lunar phases are caused by changes in how much of the sunlit side of the ________________ faces Earth.

9. Do the phases of the moon affect how much of the moon is illuminated? Explain your answer. ____
____
____
____

10. Is the following sentence true or false? The cycle of the phases takes about two days longer than the moon's revolution around Earth. ________________

11. List two reasons why the moon's surface has extremely high and low temperatures. ____
____

Eclipses

12. A(n) ________________ eclipse occurs when the moon passes between Earth and the sun and casts a shadow on Earth.

13. Is the following sentence true or false? A lunar eclipse occurs when the moon passes into Earth's shadow. ________________

14. What must happen in order for an eclipse to take place? ________________
____
____

15. Who can see a total eclipse of the moon when it occurs? ________________
____

Name ______________________ Class ________________ Date ____________

Section 22.3 Earth's Moon

This section describes the moon's structure, surface, and ideas about its origin.

Reading Strategy

As you read, complete the flowchart showing the stages leading to the formation of the moon. For more information on this Reading Strategy, see the **Reading and Study Skills** in the **Skills and Reference Handbook** at the end of your textbook.

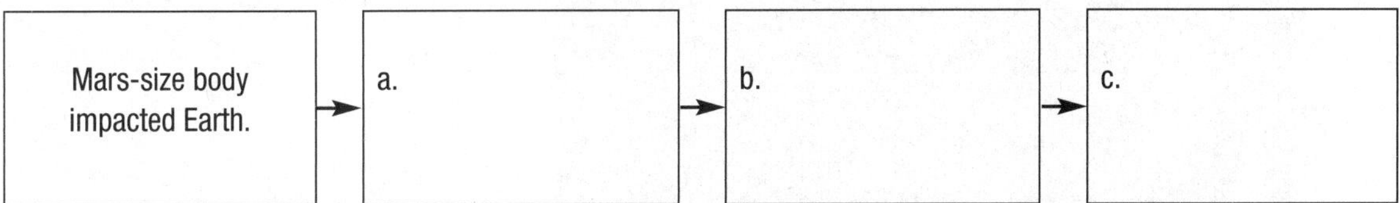

1. The density of the moon is comparable to that of mantle rocks on ______________.

The Lunar Surface

Match each description with its moon feature.

	Description	Moon Feature
_____	**2.** densely pitted, light colored areas containing mountain ranges	a. regolith
_____	**3.** dark, relatively smooth areas made of ancient beds of basaltic lava	b. maria
_____	**4.** splash marks that radiate outwards for hundreds of kilometers	c. craters
_____	**5.** long channels similar to valleys or trenches	d. rays
_____	**6.** soil-like layer of igneous rock, glass beads, and fine lunar dust	e. highlands
_____	**7.** round depressions produced by the impact of rapidly moving debris or meteoroids	f. rilles

8. How did the maria on the moon's surface form? ______________________________

____

9. Complete the table below.

Characteristic	Highlands	Maria
Color		dark
Surface texture		
Mountains present?		
Rilles present?		

10. Select the appropriate letter in the figure that identifies each of the following moon features.

_____ crater _____ highland _____ mare

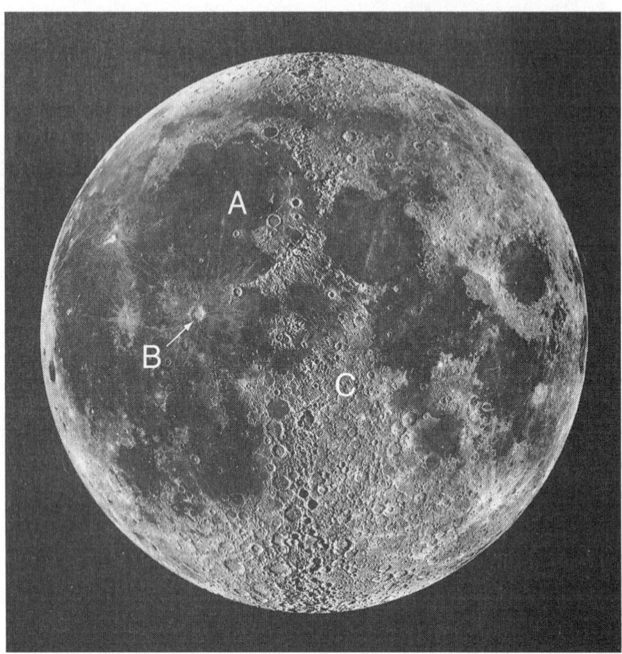

Lunar History

11. What is the most widely accepted theory of the moon's origin? ______________________________

____

____

12. The greater the density of craters on the moon, the ________________ the surface must be.

13. List the three phases in which the moon evolved in order from oldest to youngest.

a. ________________

b. ________________

c. ________________

14. Is the following sentence true or false? Lava flows on the moon sometimes overlap highlands, showing that maria deposits are younger than highlands. ________________

15. Why have very old craters on the moon not been erased as similar craters on Earth have been? ______________________________

____

____

____

Name ______________________ Class __________________ Date ____________

WordWise

Use the clues below to identify vocabulary terms from Chapter 22. Write the terms, putting one letter in each blank. Use the circled letters to find the hidden word.

Clues

1. apparent westward drift of a planet as seen from Earth
2. an oval-shaped path
3. average distance between Earth and the sun
4. spinning of a body on its axis
5. motion of a body along a path around some point in space
6. point at which Earth is farthest from the sun
7. point at which the moon is farthest from Earth
8. cycle of changes in the amount of the moon that appears lit
9. splash mark radiating outward from a crater

Vocabulary Terms

1. _ _ _ _ _ _ _ _ ◯ _ _   _ _ _ _ _ _ _
2. _ _ _ _ _ ◯ _
3. _ _ ◯ _ _ _ _ _ _ _ _ _ _ _   _ _ _ _
4. ◯ _ _ _ _ _ _ _
5. _ _ _ ◯ _ _ _ _ _ _
6. _ _ _ _ _ _ _ ◯
7. _ _ ◯ _ _ _
8. _ _ _ _ _ _   _ _   _ _ _   ◯ _ _ _
9. _ _ ◯

Hidden Word: _ _ _ _ _ _ _ _ _

Definition: ____

Section 23.1 The Solar System

This section gives an overview of the planets of the solar system and describes the nebular theory of the formation of the solar system.

Reading Strategy

Complete the flowchart on the formation of the solar system. For more information on this Reading Strategy, see the **Reading and Study Skills** in the **Skills and Reference Handbook** at the end of your textbook.

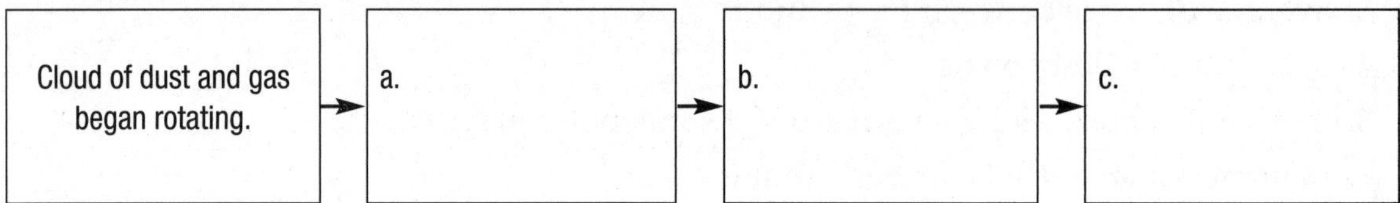

1. Almost all of the mass of the solar system is within the ________________.
2. Is the following sentence true or false? The farther a planet is from the sun, the shorter its period of revolution. ________________
3. List the planet or planets whose orbital planes lie more than 3 degrees from the plane of the sun's equator. ________________

The Planets: An Overview

4. List the main differences between the terrestrial and Jovian planets.
   a. ________________ b. ________________
   c. ________________ d. ________________
5. Indicate whether each of the following planets is a terrestrial planet or a Jovian planet.
   a. Saturn ________________
   b. Venus ________________
   c. Mercury ________________
   d. Uranus ________________
   e. Mars ________________
   f. Neptune ________________
   g. Jupiter ________________
6. The ________________ planets are relatively small and rocky.
7. Is the following sentence true or false? The Jovian planets are huge, rocky giants. ________________
8. List the groups of substances that make up the planets. ________________

____

9. Give two reasons why the Jovian planets have much thicker atmospheres than the terrestrial planets. ______________________________

____

____

10. To escape from a planet's gravity, an object must reach a speed called the ________________.

11. Complete the table below.

Characteristic	Terrestrial Planets	Jovian Planets
Comparative size		
Density (compared to water)		
Interior composition		
Atmosphere thickness		

Formation of the Solar System

12. A(n) ________________ is a cloud of dust and gas in space.

13. Describe the nebular theory of the formation of the solar system. ______________________________

____

____

14. Circle the letter of the term for small, irregularly shaped bodies.
    a. planet
    b. grain
    c. ice
    d. planetesimal

15. Is the following sentence true or false? The inner planets formed mainly from metals and silicate minerals because of the high temperatures near the sun. ________________

16. The Jovian planets contain large quantities of ices because it was ________________ enough in the outer solar system for ices to form.

Section 23.2 The Terrestrial Planets

This section describes the features of Mercury, Venus, and Mars.

Reading Strategy

Before you read, add to the web diagram properties that you already know about Mars. Then add details about each property as your read. Make a similar web diagram for each of the other terrestrial planets. For more information on this Reading Strategy, see the **Reading and Study Skills** in the **Skills and Reference Handbook** at the end of your textbook.

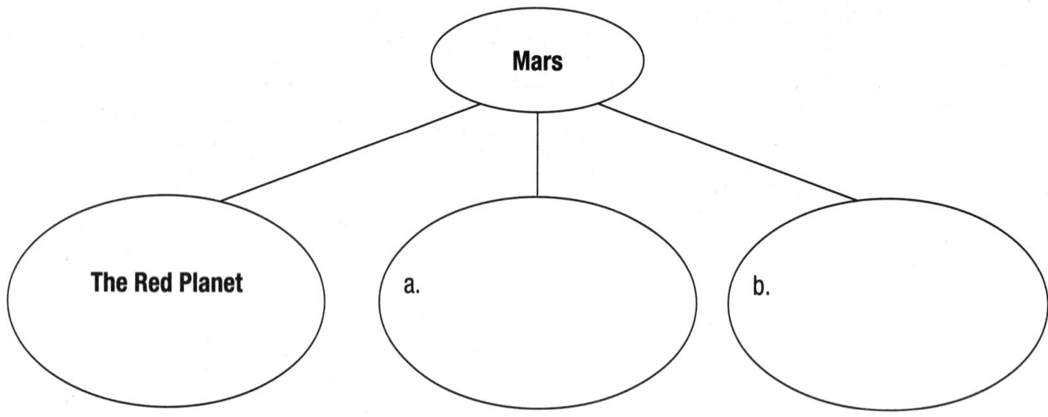

Mercury: The Innermost Planet

1. Circle the letter of Mercury's position in the solar system.
   a. innermost terrestrial planet
   b. innermost Jovian planet
   c. outermost terrestrial planet
   d. outermost Jovian planet
2. Name four ways in which Mercury is similar to the moon and two ways in which it is different.
   Similar: ____________________
   ____
   ____
   Different: ____________________
   ____
   ____
3. Mercury has the greatest ________________ extremes of any planet.
4. Why is it unlikely that life as we know it exists on Mercury?
   ____
   ____

Name ______________________ Class ________________ Date ____________

Venus: The Veiled Planet

5. List four reasons Venus is referred to as "Earth's twin."

____

____

6. Venus's topography has been mapped from space and Earth, using ________________ pulses.

7. Is the following sentence true or false? Most of Venus's surface consists of plains covered by lava flows. ________________

8. Why is it unlikely that life as we know it exists on Venus?

____

____

Mars: The Red Planet

9. Is the following sentence true or false? Mars's atmosphere is 90 times the density of Earth's. ________________

10. Circle the letter of the gas that makes up most of the Martian atmosphere.

    a. nitrogen
    b. oxygen
    c. carbon dioxide
    d. water vapor

11. Mars's polar caps are made of ________________ covered with a thin layer of frozen ________________ .

12. Color changes on Mars's surface observed from Earth may be caused by ________________ in Mars's atmosphere.

13. Is the following sentence true or false? The largest volcano on Mars is over 2 1/2 times higher than Mount Everest.

____

14. How were the large canyons on Mars thought to have formed?

____

____

15. Identify the features labeled A and B in the figure.

    A ________________

    B ________________

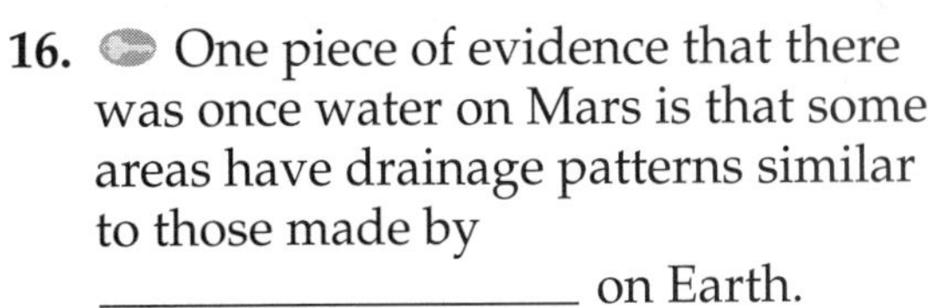

16. One piece of evidence that there was once water on Mars is that some areas have drainage patterns similar to those made by ________________ on Earth.

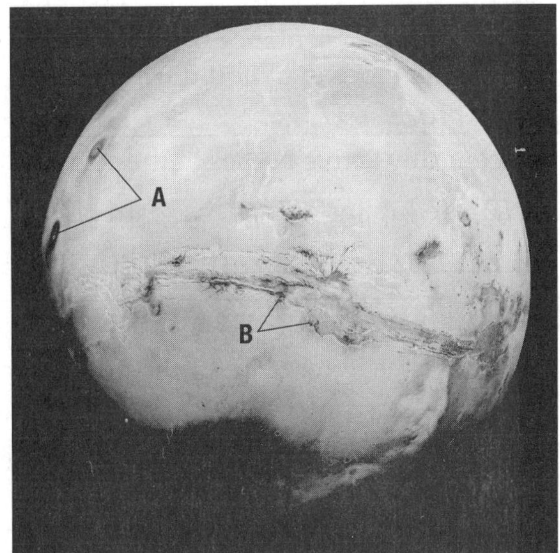

17. Is the following sentence true or false? The finding of evidence of liquid water on Mars is important because water is essential for life.

____

Name ______________________ Class ______________ Date ___________

Chapter 23 Touring Our Solar System

Section 23.3 The Outer Planets (and Pluto)

This section describes the features of Jupiter, Saturn, Uranus, Neptune, and Pluto, the dwarf planet.

Reading Strategy

In the table, write a brief summary of the characteristics of each planet. For more information on this Reading Strategy, see the **Reading and Study Skills** in the **Skills and Reference Handbook** at the end of your textbook.

Outer Planet	Characteristics
Jupiter	largest, most mass, Great Red Spot

Jupiter: Giant Among Planets

1. Circle the letter of the answer that correctly describes Jupiter's mass.
   a. 800 times as massive as the sun
   b. the same mass as the sun
   c. 2 1/2 times greater than the mass of all of the other planets and moons combined
   d. the same mass as all of the other planets and moons combined
2. Is the following sentence true or false? Jupiter's surface is thought to be a giant ocean of liquid water. ______________
3. One of Jupiter's moons, ______________, is one of only four volcanically active bodies in the solar system.
4. What are Jupiter's rings made up of? ______________________________

____

Saturn: The Elegant Planet

5. Circle the letter of Saturn's most prominent feature.
   a. moon system
   b. ring system
   c. giant storm
   d. liquid oceans

6. Describe the features of the A and B rings in the figure. ______________

____

7. Describe the features of the E rings in the figure. ______________

____

8. Is the following sentence true or false? Saturn has large cyclonic "storms" similar to Jupiter's Great Red Spot.

____

9. Circle the letter of the planet(s) that have ring systems.
   a. Saturn only
   b. Saturn and Jupiter only
   c. all four Jovian planets
   d. all eight planets

10. What unusual feature does Saturn's moon Titan share with Neptune's moon Triton? ______________

____

Uranus: The Sideways Planet

11. What is unique about Uranus's axis of rotation? ______________

____

12. Is the following sentence true or false? Uranus's rings were discovered when Uranus passed in front of a distant star and blocked its view. ______________

13. Uranus's moon Miranda has a greater variety of ______________ than any solar system body yet examined.

Neptune: The Windy Planet

14. Is the following sentence true or false? Neptune has winds exceeding 1000 km per hour. ______________

15. Circle the letter of the substance that most likely makes up Neptune's upper cloud layer.
   a. water droplets
   b. ice crystals
   c. frozen carbon dioxide
   d. frozen methane

16. What does the retrograde motion of Neptune's moon Triton indicate about its origin? ______________

____

Pluto: Dwarf Planet

17. Pluto is no longer considered to be a ______________.

18. Describe Pluto's structure. ______________

____

Section 23.4 Minor Members of the Solar System

This section describes the characteristics of asteroids, comets, and meteoroids.

Reading Strategy

As you read this section, write a definition for each vocabulary term in your own words and enter it in the table. For more information on this Reading Strategy, see the **Reading and Study Skills** in the **Skills and Reference Handbook** at the end of your textbook.

Vocabulary	Definition
asteroid	

Asteroids

1. Is the following sentence true or false? Asteroids are small, rocky bodies in space. ____________________

2. Where are most asteroids found? ____
____

3. Asteroids cannot be the remains of a broken planet because they do not have enough total ____________________.

Comets

4. ____________________ are pieces of rocky and metallic materials held together by frozen gases.

5. Circle the letter of the term for the glowing head of a comet formed when frozen gases vaporize.
   a. nucleus
   b. coma
   c. gas tail
   d. dust tail

6. Select the appropriate letter in the figure that identifies each of the following parts of a comet.

   _____ nucleus

   _____ tail of ionized gases

   _____ coma

   _____ tail of dust

7. When do comets develop tails? ____
____

8. List the two regions from which comets originate. _______________________
____

9. Is the following sentence true or false? The nucleus of Halley's comet is spherical. ________________

Meteoroids

Match each description with its object.

	Description	Object
_____	10. small, solid particle from space that reaches Earth's surface	a. meteor
_____	11. small, solid particle from space that burns up in Earth's atmosphere	b. meteoroid
_____	12. small, solid particle that travels through space	c. meteorite

13. List the three sources of most meteoroids. ________________
____
____
____
____

14. A(n) ________________, or display of frequent meteor sightings, can result when Earth encounters a swarm of meteoroids.

15. What is the origin of large craters on Earth such as Meteor Crater in Arizona? ____
____
____

16. Is the following sentence true or false? Meteorites are now the only extraterrestrial materials scientists have to examine directly.

____

Section 24.1 The Study of Light

This section describes the electromagnetic spectrum and how scientists use spectroscopy to study it. It also explains the Doppler effect and how it is used in astronomy.

Reading Strategy

Before you read, predict the meaning of the term *electromagnetic spectrum* and write your definition in the table. After you read, revise your definition if it was incorrect. For more information on this Reading Strategy, see the **Reading and Study Skills** in the **Skills and Reference Handbook** at the end of your textbook.

Vocabulary Term	Before You Read	After You Read
electromagnetic spectrum	a.	b.

1. Why is an understanding of light important to astronomers? _______________

____

____

Electromagnetic Radiation

2. The arrangement of electromagnetic waves according to their wavelengths and frequencies is called the _______________.

3. List the types of energy that make up the electromagnetic spectrum.

____

____

____

4. Is the following sentence true or false? Different electromagnetic waves travel through vacuum at different speeds.

____

5. Circle the letter of the best description of the nature of light.

a Light always behaves like waves.

b. Light always behaves like particles.

c. Light sometimes behaves like waves and at other times like particles.

d. Light never behaves like either waves or particles.

Name ______________ Class ______________ Date ______________

6. How can you show that visible light is made up of many different wavelengths?
____
____

7. Particles of light are called ______________.

8. According to the figure, how are frequency and wavelength related? ____
____

9. Circle the letter of the waves in the figure that have the highest frequency.
   a. gamma rays
   b. ultraviolet rays
   c. infrared rays
   d. radio waves

Spectroscopy

Match each description with its spectrum.

Description	Spectrum
_____ 10. band of color with a series of dark lines running through it	a. absorption spectrum
_____ 11. uninterrupted band of color	b. emission spectrum
_____ 12. series of bright lines of particular wavelengths	c. continuous spectrum

13. Spectroscopy is the study of the properties of light that depend on ______________.

14. What can a star's spectrum tell astronomers about the star? ______________
____

The Doppler Effect

15. When a wave source is moving toward or away from an object, the wavelength changes, a phenomenon known as the ______________.

Match each situation with its type of change in a wave.

Situation	Change in Wave
_____ 16. sound source approaches an observer	a. pitch becomes lower
_____ 17. light source moves away from an observer	b. pitch becomes higher
_____ 18. sound source moves away from an observer	c. light becomes bluer
_____ 19. light source approaches an observer	d. light becomes redder

20. How is the Doppler effect used in astronomy? ______________
____

Section 24.2 Tools for Studying Space

This section describes refracting, reflecting, radio, and space telescopes and how they work.

Reading Strategy

As you read, complete the Venn diagram below to show the differences between refracting and reflecting telescopes. For more information on this Reading Strategy, see the **Reading and Study Skills** in the **Skills and Reference Handbook** at the end of your textbook.

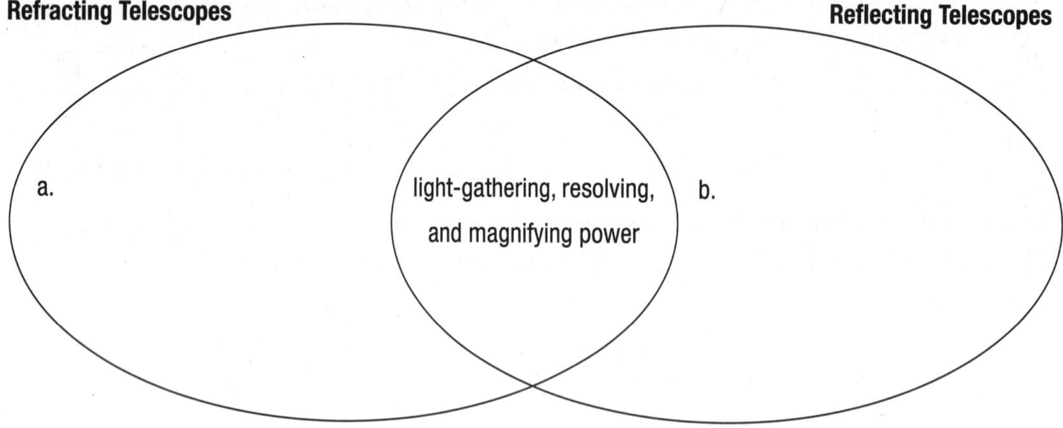

Refracting Telescopes

1. What is the function of the objective lens of a refracting telescope? ______________________________

____

____

2. Select the appropriate letter in the figure that identifies each of the following features.

_____ objective lens
_____ focus
_____ focal length of the objective
_____ eyepiece
_____ focal length of the eyepiece

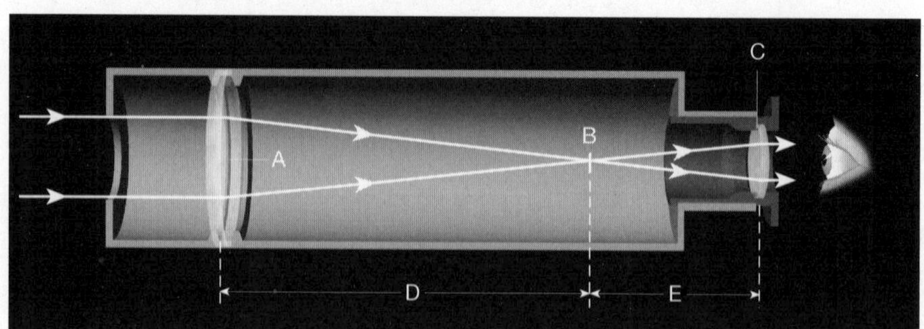

3. Refracting telescopes got their name because they refract, or ______________, light.

4. Is the following sentence true or false? Astronomers usually study an object by looking directly through a telescope. ________________

5. Is the following sentence true or false? Refracting telescopes suffer from an optical defect called chromatic aberration. ________________

Reflecting Telescopes

6. The main difference between a reflecting telescope and a refracting telescope is that a reflecting telescope uses a(n) ________________ to focus the incoming light.

7. Is the following sentence true or false? Most large optical telescopes are reflectors. ________________

8. List three properties of optical telescopes that aid astronomers in their work. ____

____

Detecting Invisible Radiation

9. Circle the letter of the type of invisible radiation from space that can be detected from Earth's surface.

   a. gamma rays
   b. X-rays
   c. infrared radiation
   d. radio waves

10. Is the following sentence true or false? A radio telescope works in a similar way to a radio antenna. ________________

11. Why is it not necessary for radio telescope surfaces to be as smooth as a mirror? ____

____

12. List five advantages of radio telescopes over optical telescopes.

____

____

____

____

Space Telescopes

13. Why do space telescopes produce clearer images than telescopes on Earth?

____

____

14. Circle the letter of the first space telescope.

   a. Hubble Space Telescope
   b. Chandra X-ray Observatory
   c. Compton Gamma-Ray Observatory
   d. James Webb Space Telescope

15. Is the following sentence true or false? Different space telescopes collect the same information about an object in space.

____

Section 24.3 The Sun

This section describes the structure of the sun, features on the sun's surface, and nuclear fusion in the interior of the sun.

Reading Strategy

Preview the Key Concepts, topic headings, vocabulary, and figures in this section. In the table, list two things you expect to learn. After reading, complete the table, stating what you have learned about each item you listed. For more information on this Reading Strategy, see the **Reading and Study Skills** in the **Skills and Reference Handbook** at the end of your textbook.

What I Expect to Learn	What I Learned
a.	b.
c.	d.

Structure of the Sun

1. List the four main parts of the sun. ______________________________

____

____

2. What is the solar wind? ______________________________

____

____

Match each description with its sun layer.

	Description	Sun Layer
_____	3. outermost part of the sun's atmosphere	a. chromosphere
_____	4. relatively thin layer of the sun's atmosphere	b. photosphere
_____	5. layer that radiates most of the sunlight we can see	c. corona

Name ______________________ Class ________________ Date ___________

6. Select the appropriate letter in the figure that identifies each of the following features.

   _____ prominence

   _____ chromosphere

   _____ sunspots

   _____ corona

   _____ core

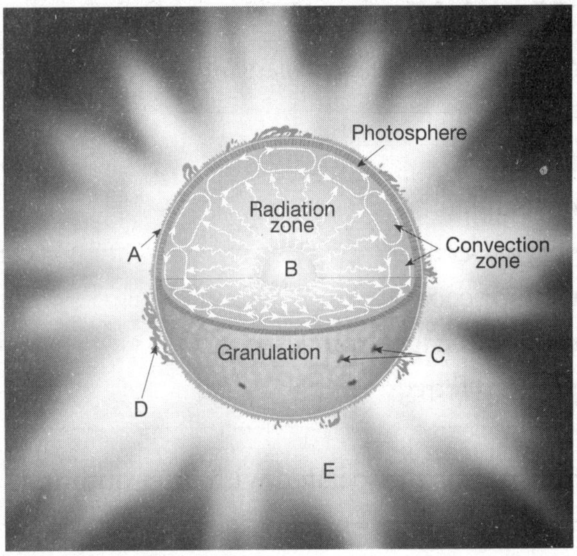

The Active Sun

Match each description with its sun feature.

	Description	Sun Feature
_____	7. dark region on the surface of the photosphere	a. solar flare
_____	8. brief outburst associated with sunspot clusters	b. sunspot
_____	9. huge cloudlike structure of chromospheric gases	c. prominence

10. Is the following sentence true or false? Different parts of the sun rotate at different speeds. ________________

11. Why do sunspots appear dark? ______________________________

____

12. Prominences are ionized gases trapped by ________________ extending from regions of intense solar activity.

13. List the main forms of radiation in which solar flares release energy.

____

14. Solar flares can cause spectacular ________________, or northern and southern lights, in Earth's atmosphere.

The Solar Interior

15. Is the following sentence true or false? The sun produces energy by nuclear fission. ________________

16. During nuclear fusion, ________________ is converted into energy.

17. In what form is most of the energy from hydrogen fusion released?

____

18. The sun became hot enough to start nuclear fusion because the temperature of gases rises when they are ________________.

Name ______________________ Class ________________ Date ____________

WordWise

Complete the sentences by using the scrambled vocabulary terms below.

ntooshp	noraoc
nostsups	odiar clpesoeet
eptyrossccop	osnniuotuc mtecrpus
rhhtoppeeos	roals rslefa
mlceentrocageti tpmecsru	etagncirfr eceletpso
plodrep fetfec	

Sunspots are associated with brief outbursts called ____________________.

____________________ are dark regions on the surface of the photosphere.

The study of the properties of light that depend on wavelength is ____________________.

A(n) ____________________ uses wire mesh as a reflector to collect radiation from space.

The siren from an ambulance that is approaching you seems louder because of the ____________________.

Galileo used a(n) ____________________that had a lens to bend light.

The ____________________ is the outermost part of the sun's atmosphere.

Most of the sunlight we can see comes from the ____________________ of the sun.

The ____________________ is the arrangement of electromagnetic waves according to their wavelengths and frequencies.

____________________ are particles of light.

An uninterrupted band of color produced by a prism is a(n) ____________________.

Name ______________ Class ______________ Date ______________

Section 25.1 Properties of Stars

This section describes the characteristics of stars, explains how astronomers measure distances to stars, and describes the Hertzprung-Russell diagram.

Reading Strategy

Before you read, write two questions about the Hertzprung-Russell diagram on page 704. As you read, write answers to your questions. For more information on this Reading Strategy, see the **Reading and Study Skills** in the **Skills and Reference Handbook** at the end of your textbook.

Questions About the Hertzprung-Russell Diagram	
Question	**Answer**
a.	b.
c.	d.

Characteristics of Stars

1. List three properties of stars. ______________

2. Is the following sentence true or false? A star's color can tell you what its approximate temperature is. ______________

3. What are binary stars? ______________

4. Binary stars can be used to determine the ______________ of a star.

Measuring Distances to Stars

5. The apparent change in position of a star when seen from opposite sides of Earth's orbit is called ______________.

6. Circle the letter of each statement that is true.
   a. Nearby stars have large parallax angles.
   b. Nearby stars have larger parallax angles than distant stars have.
   c. All stars have measurable parallax angles.
   d. The parallax angles of distant stars are too small to measure.

7. Is the following sentence true or false? Astronomers have calculated the parallax angles of millions of stars. ______________

8. What is a light-year? ______________

Name ____________________ Class ____________________ Date ____________

Stellar Brightness

9. List three factors that control the apparent brightness of a star as seen from Earth. ______________________________

____

10. Is the following sentence true or false? A third-magnitude star is ten times as bright as a fourth-magnitude star.

____

Match each definition to its term.

	Definition	Term
_____	11. a star's brightness as it appears from Earth	a. absolute magnitude
_____	12. how bright a star actually is	b. apparent magnitude

13. The star Arcturus has a much greater absolute magnitude than the sun but a much lower apparent magnitude. Why is this? ______________________________

____

____

Hertzsprung-Russell Diagram

14. Circle the letter of what a Hertzsprung-Russell diagram shows.
   a. the location of stars in the sky
   b. the absolute magnitude and temperature of stars
   c. the apparent magnitude and temperature of stars
   d. the absolute magnitude and mass of stars

15. About ______________ percent of stars are main-sequence stars.

16. Select the appropriate letter in the figure that identifies each of the following features.

_____ the sun

_____ cool, small, red stars

_____ white dwarfs (small faint stars)

_____ red giants (bright cool stars)

_____ hot, large, blue stars

Idealized Hertzsprung-Russell Diagram

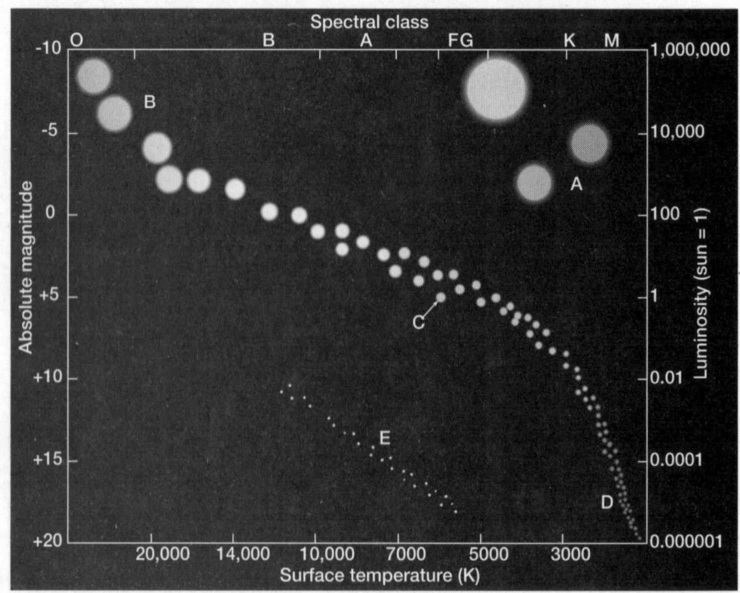

Name ______________ Class ______________ Date ______________

Section 25.2 Stellar Evolution

This section describes the evolution of stars from birth to burnout and death. It also discusses types of stellar remnants.

Reading Strategy

As you read, complete the flowchart to show how the sun evolves. Expand the chart to show the evolution of low-mass and high-mass stars. For more information on this Reading Strategy, see the **Reading and Study Skills** in the **Skills and Reference Handbook** at the end of your textbook.

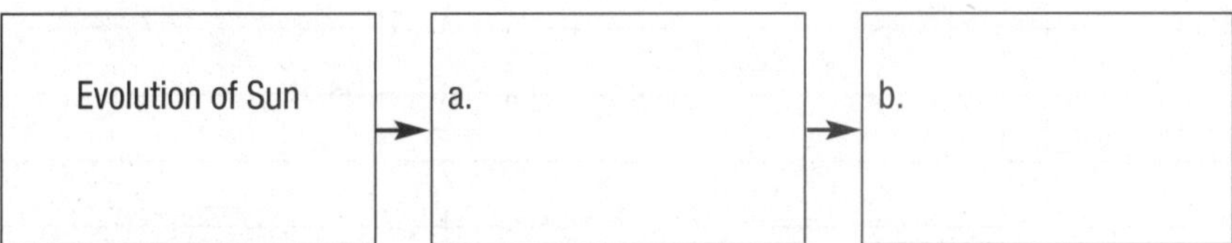

Star Birth

1. What is the process by which a star is born? ______________

2. List in order the labeled stages shown on the figure that a medium-mass star goes through during its "life." (*Hint:* it may be helpful to draw arrows on the figure from stage to stage.)

a. ______________ e. ______________

b. ______________ f. ______________

c. ______________ g. ______________

d. ______________ h. ______________

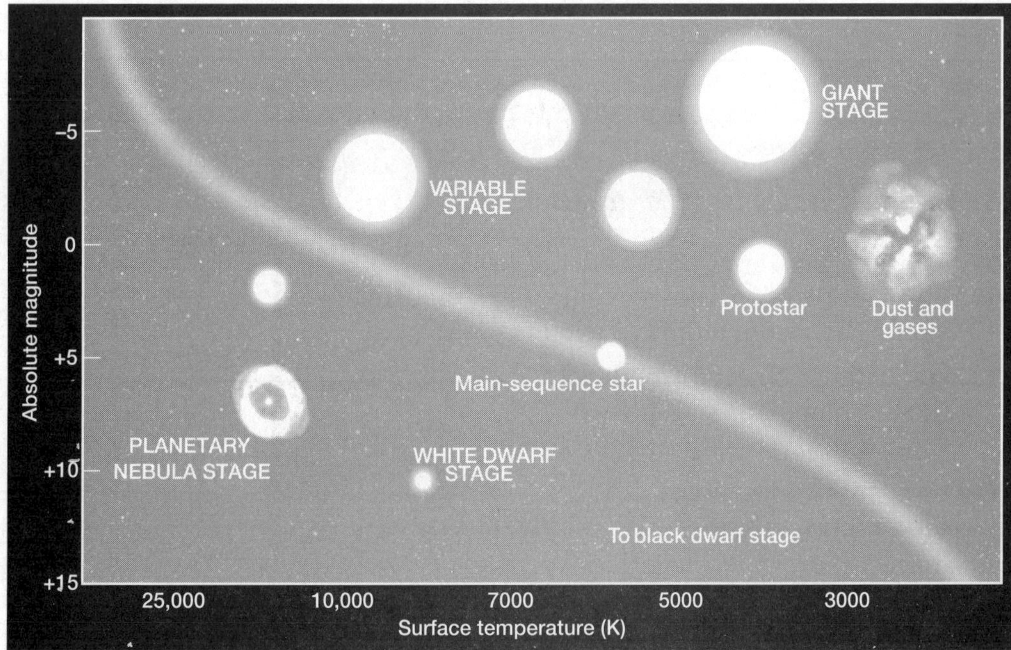

3. A(n) ________________ is a developing star not yet hot enough to engage in nuclear fusion.
4. Is the following sentence true or false? An average star spends 90 percent of its life as a helium-burning main-sequence star. ________________

Burnout and Death

5. Is the following sentence true or false? All stars eventually run out of fuel and collapse due to gravity. ________________
6. How can a Hertzsprung-Russell diagram be used to show the evolution of a star? ____

____

____

____

Match each death description with its star.

	Death Description	Star
_____	7. forms a red giant, which then collapses into a red dwarf and forms a planetary nebula	a. low-mass star
_____	8. blows up in a supernova explosion	b. medium-mass star
_____	9. does not form a red giant; collapses directly into a white dwarf	c. massive star

Stellar Remnants

10. List the stages the sun has gone through and will go through during its evolution. ____

____

____

11. A(n) ________________ is a neutron star that rotates and generates radio waves.

Match each description with its stellar remnant.

	Description	Stellar Remnant
_____	12. remnant of a supernova event; similar to a large atomic nucleus	a. black hole
_____	13. small dense object formed from the remnants of a star at least three times as massive as the sun	b. white dwarf
_____	14. remnant of a low-mass or medium-mass star	c. neutron star

Name ______________________ Class ______________ Date __________

Section 25.3 The Universe

This section describes the Milky Way galaxy and types of galaxies. It also explains how we know the universe is expanding, how the universe probably began, and how it might end.

Reading Strategy

As you read, complete the outline of the most important ideas in this section. For more information on this Reading Strategy, see the **Reading and Study Skills** in the **Skills and Reference Handbook** at the end of your textbook.

I. The Universe
- A. Milky Way Galaxy
  - 1. ______________________
  - 2. ______________________
- B. ______________________
  - 1. Spiral Galaxy ______________________
  - 2. Elliptical Galaxy ______________________
  - 3. ______________________
  - 4. ______________________

____

____

____

1. A(n) ______________ is a large group of stars, dust, and gases held together by gravity.

The Milky Way Galaxy

2. Why is it difficult to study the Milky Way Galaxy, using optical telescopes?

____

3. Circle the letter of the type of galaxy that the Milky Way is.

   a. spiral galaxy
   b. elliptical galaxy
   c. irregular galaxy
   d. cluster galaxy

Types of Galaxies

Match each description with its galaxy.

	Description	Galaxy
_____	4. ranges in shape from round to oval; most are small	a. spiral
_____	5. composed mostly of young stars	b. elliptical
_____	6. usually disk-shaped with many variations	c. irregular

7. Is the following sentence true or false? The disk of the Milky Way Galaxy is about 100,000 light-years wide and about 10,000 light-years thick at the nucleus. ____________

8. A(n) ____________ of thin gas and clusters of stars surrounds the disk of the Milky Way Galaxy.

9. Galaxies are not distributed randomly but are grouped in ____________.

10. The larger galaxy in the photograph is a(n) ____________ galaxy.

11. Is the following sentence true or false? The larger galaxy in the photograph probably contains mostly young stars. ____________

The Expanding Universe

12. Is the following sentence true or false? The Doppler effect can tell us whether a galaxy is moving toward or away from us. ____________

13. Most galaxies have Doppler shifts toward the ____________ end of the spectrum.

14. What is Hubble's law? ____________

15. The red shifts of distant galaxies show that the universe is ____________.

The Big Bang

16. Is the following sentence true or false? All distant galaxies are moving away from ours because our galaxy is at the center of the universe. ____________

17. The ____________ theory states that the universe began when a dense, hot, supermassive ball violently exploded.

18. Circle the letter of each item that is evidence for the big bang theory.
    a. red shift of galaxies
    b. supernova explosions
    c. cosmic background radiation
    d. galactic clusters

19. Describe two possible ways the universe might end. ____________